The Critical Idiom

Founder Editor: JOHN D. JUMP (1969–1976)

12 Plot

In the same series

Plot / *Elizabeth Dipple*

Methuen & Co Ltd

First published 1970
by Methuen & Co Ltd
11 New Fetter Lane, London EC4P 4EE
Reprinted 1977

© 1970 Elizabeth Dipple

Printed in Great Britain
by J. W. Arrowsmith Ltd, Bristol

ISBN 0 416 19780 9

Distributed in the U.S.A. by
HARPER & ROW PUBLISHERS, INC.
BARNES & NOBLE IMPORT DIVISION

Contents

General Editor's Preface

The volumes composing the Critical Idiom deal with a wide variety of key terms in our critical vocabulary. The purpose of the series differs from that served by the standard glossaries of literary terms. Many terms are adequately defined for the needs of students by the brief entries in these glossaries, and such terms do not call for attention in the present series. But there are other terms which cannot be made familiar by means of compact definitions. Students need to grow accustomed to them through simple and straightforward but reasonably full discussions. The main purpose of this series is to provide such discussions.

Many critics have borrowed methods and criteria from currently influential bodies of knowledge or belief that have developed without particular reference to literature. In our own century, some of them have drawn on art-history, psychology, or sociology. Others, strong in a comprehensive faith, have looked at literature and literary criticism from a Marxist or a Christian or some other sharply defined point of view. The result has been the importation into literary criticism of terms from the vocabularies of these sciences and creeds. Discussions of such bodies of knowledge and belief in their bearing upon literature and literary criticism form a natural extension of the initial aim of the Critical Idiom.

Because of their diversity of subject-matter, the studies in the series vary considerably in structure. But all authors have tried to give as full illustrative quotation as possible, to make reference whenever appropriate to more than one literature, and to write in such a way as to guide readers towards the short bibliographies in which they have made suggestions for further reading.

University of Manchester   John D. Jump

I
Plot:
The Basic Problem

Plot currently has no strong place in the pantheon of acceptable literary terms. As a word, it has, in fact, been out of fashion since the anthropocentric surge of Romantic thought when the freedom to write plotlessly was, at least apparently, urged: the composing artist found various metaphors for himself such as that of the aeolian lyre being played upon by the spiritual wind of inspiration, but he was above all not an artisan arranging action according to a tight causal pattern of beginning, middle and end. Tristram Shandy as narrator expresses his freedom with characteristic bluntness: 'I should beg Mr Horace's pardon – for in writing what I have set about I shall confine myself neither to his rules, nor to any man's rules that ever lived.' From the eighteenth century to the present, plot has had an automatic association with rules – those rules begun so expansively by Aristotle's apparent extrapolations from Greek drama and epic and narrowed so stringently by theoretical criticism of Aristotle, Horace and Plato in the late fifteenth, sixteenth and seventeenth centuries in Italy and to a more limited extent in France and England.

The problem throughout has been one of reduction. Aristotle's style is sparse although the Greek nouns he uses are highly reverberative, and his words can be given a narrow literalness which is critically very unrewarding indeed. In certain ways the Italian theorists making their 'rules' about plot reduced Aristotle as they thought to expand him, and we are the unfortunate sufferers in that we tend to have received both Aristotle and Horace through these transmitters. Alain Robbe-Grillet offers a healthy and much needed antidote to all such projections of authority – ancient, Renaissance, or modern – when he says that no work of art should have a traditionally prescribed pattern but must search out its own form and newness. It is crucial to point out that this does not imply that literature (in this case, the novel) must be plotless, but only that each work must seek its own plan.

Reduction in our thinking about plot also has other, less venerable causes. In some ways plot projects an almost industrial idea, in that it has affinities with the graph, the blueprint and all of the stalest, least interesting diagrams of human order of one sort or another. Almost everything from statistical analyses of the stock market to the Genesis account of God's six days of creation can be graphed, plotted, seen as part of an orderly plan and superficially understood in this way. This view of plot is necessarily without literary, moral or symbolic value and is artistically unsatisfying: it has a non-literary inclusiveness which is quite repugnant to the mysteries of our trade. When a transference is made from this idea of plot as mathematical graph to literature, the most reduced form is the murder mystery in which every piece of data, both thing and event, is fitted into a jigsaw puzzle arrangement which is unravelled with precision at the end. We read murder mysteries not as a creative literary act, but as something like a means of testing our IQ – and surely a literary term should encompass more than that.

Finally, there is something primordial about plot: plot, the story, what happens next, is what we were interested in as children and what was understood in terms of the fairy tale formula which began 'Once upon a time . . .' and ended 'And they lived happily ever after'. Compulsively, when we become men, we put away childish things. This compulsion is beyond literary history and can be controlled only by expanding the term which has been so reduced, by going first of all back to the resonances of Aristotle's *mythos* and *praxis* (*mythos* can generally be translated directly as plot and *praxis* as action, although the two are often synonymous or nearly so) and carrying them through literature to what modern writers and critics understand by the energy, the action in time, and informing movement of ideas.

Essentially, the word plot carries a heavy meaning, as it comprises all action in any literary genre. This means that it must go beyond scene or incident and account, to some degree at least, for the movement of mind or soul in poems or psychological novels. If we are to give the term its due as *mythos* accompanied by *praxis*, it should be seen to contain both exterior and interior action: it is the primary term whose ramifications imply the whole art of constructing temporal progression in art. In other words, it can be argued that Aristotle was not stuffy but quite right when he claimed that, of the six constituent aspects of tragedy – plot, character, diction, thought, spectacle, and song – plot is the most important because happiness or unhappiness depends on action and life. E. M. Forster, in *Aspects of the Novel*, dismisses plot and says suavely that Aristotle was simply wrong. He then goes on to say that, as all inheritors of the tradition of the novel must know, it is character, not plot, which is the informing energy behind at least that particular genre. Rooted in his essay, however, is the assumption that we are watching the characters *in action*, moving through experience and thought to new growth and new postures. That action must be plotted by the novelist, and understood by the reader as planned and arranged according to the end the novelist has in view.

Henry James had a more inclusive instinct than Forster when he claimed the interchangeability of plot and character:

What is character but the determination of incident? What is incident but the illustration of character? What is either a picture or a novel that is *not* of character? What else do we seek in it and find in it? It is an incident for a woman to stand up with her hand resting on a table and look at you in a certain way; or if it be not an incident I think it will be hard to say what it is. At the same time it is an expression of character. If you say you don't see it (character in *that* – *allons donc!*), this is exactly what the artist who has reasons of his own for thinking he *does* see it undertakes to show you ... the only classification of the novel that I can understand is into that which has life and that which has not.

(*The Art of Fiction*, p. 405)

Notice James's assumption that the arrangement of incident (and hence the creation of *life*) is intentional as the writer tries to draw his reader where he wants him. We may perhaps dislike this controlling tyranny of the artist, but it is impossible to deny that it is there – unless we believe Yeats and go in for automatic writing. Even that, unfortunately, is plotted, if by a divine mind.

It will be the task of this monograph to trace the two and contrary ways of considering this literary word. Firstly, we must see it as it was understood by Aristotle and then progressively reduced through neo-classicism to that point which allows Edith Wharton's forthright rejection of it in her author's manual:

The double plot has long since vanished, and the 'plot' itself, in the sense of an elaborate puzzle into which a given number of characters have to be arbitrarily fitted, has gone with it to the lumber-room of discarded conventions.

(*The Writing of Fiction*, p. 82)

Secondly, we will examine the ingenious methods by which the idea of plot has been expanded in modern criticism through a proliferation of critical terms clustering around a vital idea of *poiesis*, and through the development of time theories, both literary and philosophical, which fulsomely describe the action of creation.

2

The Plot and Mimesis

At the root of Aristotle's thinking in the *Poetics* is *mimesis* – that is, imitation or representation. The implication of this stress is far-reaching, in that it claims kinship with all art forms which take as their primary energy any kind of parallelism with life. Most Western literature would fall into this large category, and even the surge towards realistic *tranche de vie* writing must lie close beside it. The literary manifestoes of realism in the nineteenth century by Belinsky, Desnoyers, the brothers Goncourt and countless others, with its philosophic expression by Hippolyte Taine, can find no true way out of the basic knowledge that Aristotle's thesis contains – namely, that the poet has not written history but a fictive artifice. The word *mimesis* applies to realism, because such writers as Balzac, Zola, and Dreiser have imitated life, perhaps more strenuously and, as they certainly hoped, more honestly than before. The real difference lies in the formal limitation of action: Aristotle allows the fiction at its best only one action and stresses its unified presentation. For him, the task of art (including painting which he says would be incapable of giving real pleasure were it not formal and representational) is architectural – the building of a possible action through skilful selection. Realism insists that life is multiform and must be rendered not singly but in its puzzling multiplicity.

The most interesting rebellion against the fictional forms which Erich Auerbach includes in his analyses of the mimetic tradition in western literature is surely that of the 'new novelists' of the 1950's and '60's in France. In *Towards a New Novel* (*Vers un Nouveau Roman*), Alain Robbe-Grillet, their most eloquent spokesman, takes up the sword against analogy and hence, it could be supposed, against *mimesis* which is primarily analogical. Art is *like* life; it is life clarified by superb presentation. But curiously, this is not Robbe-Grillet's target at all. His vigorous writing reflects preoccupations quite similar to those of Aristotle, and what he attacks is diseased narration. He would have an action delivered to the reader whole (at one point he breaks down and asserts that he does indeed have a plot, had his critics eyes to see it) but without controlling adjectival stress – that is, without the stale point-of-view manipulation on the part of a narrator who denies the reader's participation in the work's creation. This latter kind of writer supplies dangerously connotative adverbs, adjectives and homocentric comparisons which make a thing take on emotional qualities which, in fact, it does not possess. Robbe-Grillet's point is phenomenological, thing-centred; the action is there, but obscured. The reader must create it himself in the dynamics of architectural reading. As a result of objective, non-adjectival writing, a new grasp of reality should be attained.

Because we have all been conditioned by the persuasive qualities of various kinds of novelistic narrators, Robbe-Grillet's attitude at first appears bizarre, but we might remember that Aristotle mentions participation in dramatic rather than narrated art. In the *mimesis* of tragedy, we *see* the representation of reality and comprehend its wholeness while the action is mimetically taking place. This demands, logically, spontaneous participation and creativity from the audience. Like Robbe-Grillet, Aristotle suggests that the real action (Robbe-Grillet would probably find this too connotative a word and substitute 'thing') be held constantly before the mind's eye during composition so that true verisimilitude can be accomplished. The 'new novelists' are going back to certain bare features of dramatic art in trying to achieve a narrative form which denies the narrator and stresses the object. Some of this is not new, as we have been told for generations that the narrator disappeared with the advent of the twentieth century, but the stripping of humanist emotion from the forms of art and the assertion of a radical art-for-art's sake cult certainly are.

This kind of *mimesis* is probably in closest alignment with the camera and has two principal sources: it is a refined development of the realistic movement, and it participates in the bombardment of ear and eye by the new electronic mass media whose prophet is Marshall McLuhan. Although it would seem an inevitable step from the objective, toneless description of things to the depiction of those things on the screen through the medium of the camera, Robbe-Grillet insists that this representation of reality must be kept in the novel because the film is too fast for the proper comprehension which this new-old art requires. His theory has, nevertheless, gone on film in *Last Year at Marienbad*, in which all the permutations and combinations of an obscure sequence are displayed under the subtle, composing eye of Resnais's camera. If he is indeed the mouthpiece of a new theory and if this film is better than his novels as many believe, then he is probably wrong when he insists upon the continuation of linear literary modes in the dehumanized, unsentimental world which McLuhan has proclaimed and which his ideas support.

One conclusion which emerges clearly even from such a short, breathless telescoping of centuries is the continuity of the idea of *mimesis*, in spite of the changes of taste which have led to the popularity of different genres in different periods of time. Aristotle favoured tragedy as the major mimetic genre, but epic and its subsidiary, romance, took over until the Renaissance rebirth of dramatic forms, and the novel was in the ascendancy until the mid-twentieth century when film and its electronic aids appear to have taken over. This shifting emphasis does not deny the concurrent validity of other genres: neither stage drama, poem, nor novel is dead, but the popular consumer's eyes have gone elsewhere. And, of, course, Aristotle cared also about epic and even the low mimetic forms of comedy. Action is continually present to be imitated, and we may suppose that a major form of art and many minor ones will seize the opportunity, working out their plots or composition according to the tools of the medium.

As Aristotle wrote, he apparently extrapolated his descriptions from particular examples, but he nevertheless set up general and absolute rules towards which, in his logic, the particulars have always reached and which they will always support. He is therefore an arbiter, speaking generously but firmly about the oughtness of literary composition. This aspect makes him both dangerous and suspect to the modern mind which is more Ramistic in its logic. The Ramist works constantly from particular to general: the particular is prior to the general, and the latter is always subject to change or modification as the particulars accumulate. The difference between Aristotelian and Ramistic logic presents a metaphor for our thinking about the development of plotted or geometric literature. As moderns, we believe in infinite levels of change, and rebel against the idea of rules which imply that a certain potentiality may be realized and a static plateau reached. Regardless of the value of an arbiter's words, there can be no final doctrine. Interestingly, Aristotle's appeal nevertheless remains extensive because his text can trick us into believing that he has only extrapolated, that Sophocles and Euripides taught him about tragedy, Homer about epic, and that he is therefore a helpful ancient on whose shoulders we can stand to see farther.

The fact is that his theoretical regulations provide what Matthew Arnold called a touchstone. He gave literature the word plot and explained what it is – a task much more daring and important than anything achieved by Plato's few references to literature or by the witty, cautious examination of *decorum* and disposition presented by Horace in the *Ars Poetica*. In discussing Robbe-Grillet's ideas,

I have tried to indicate both continuity and differentiation in literary and aesthetic theory. Aristotle's rules for plotting may no longer retain an aura of the absolute, but they are intelligent and far-reaching. It is surely important to learn to walk in that school before we take up dancing.

A man is called a poet not because he makes verses, claims Aristotle (section 9), but because he makes plots through the representation of action: *mythos, mimesis, praxis*, the three inseparables. His essential task is to present universals rather than particulars, a task which elevates his work to the level of philosophical achievement and places him above the historian who can deal only in particulars. If he chooses to write history, his narration will be separated from that of the mere historian through the fact that he selects according to the laws of possibility and probability, and he will remain a poet.

But, as Aristotle is well aware, a plot is not an easy thing to achieve with appropriate success, although the accumulation of literature even as early as his experience reveals a vast plethora of attempts. When the poet has attained the method of creating pleasure or beauty, his presentation will be understood primarily as having a beginning, a middle, and an end. It will be a complex *mythos*, rather than simple: that is, it will contain a reversal (*peripeteia*) or a recognition (*anagnorisis*), or both. If it is a tragedy, it will end in a calamity brought about by the structure of action or the interior flaw (*hamartia*) of the character who falls.

These characteristics will be evident in the completed work of art, but the poet must think not only of product but of process as well. While writing, he must try to keep the scene before his eyes so that the maximum perfection can be reached in his representation. The poet, like the philosopher, should work from general to particular, planning first a general outline of the action, and then filling it in and expanding it by working out the proper episodes, relatively short for tragedy, relatively long for epic.

Regardless of genre, the action must be easily contained in the mind and not escape into episodic confusion. In devising the beginning, middle, and end, the tragic poet actually depends on two movements – complication and denouement (catastrophe), of the knitting and unravelling of the action. This, in skeleton, is the art of process, and it is surely much less satisfying than his exposition of the qualities of the product.

As he instructs, Aristotle may be accused of omission – especially by a modern audience which is obsessed with process – or rather we may say that he fails to give the descriptions that we require. Between the knitting and the unravelling, for example, comes the point of change to good or bad fortune. Although Aristotle insists that the poet must be equally expert at both rising and falling action (to borrow from Fortune's wheel), he is silent on the nature and precise placing of the crisis or watershed of the action – that moment which institutes what Suzanne Langer has called 'the tragic rhythm', and which constitutes the turn – the moment between rising and falling, between knitting and unravelling. Mechanically, we can take the route of the Renaissance Italian critics who held to Horace's five-act structure and contended that in the ideal play, the complication would take two and a half acts, and the denouement the other two and a half, so that the crisis is simply a straightforward reversal which happens in dead centre of the temporal progression of the plot. Chiefly, however, it is clear that interpretation is necessary. It is not enough to set a writer down with such spare instructions how to do it, as the Italian theorists of the Cinquecento well knew, and as all subsequent literary theory reflects.

Aristotle's *Poetics* did not die but only slept through the Middle Ages, and the rhetoricians, deriving their traditions ultimately from Cicero and Quintilian, taught the poet how to write, to plot, to arrange action. As E. R. Curtius has shown, topics (*topoi*) or formulae often dictated methods of filling up a structure largely fore-ordained by the rules of antique rhetoric (Chapter 5). More-over, because the active force of the medieval period was Judaeo-Christian, a change in the style of *mimesis* gradually took place, severing the classical distinction between high and low styles. Auerbach describes a new kind of realism in which high and low can be dissolved because of their resolution in the person of Christ – king of kings, born in a stable, subjected to the degradation of a very shoddy method of public execution. For Augustine and subsequent Fathers, more crucial visions were possible and led to a vertical figural interpretation of history. Just as Adam and Isaac prefigured Christ, so each event in history or literature may be seen as a figural representation of an aspect of divine revelation. The classical idea ran contrary to this and involved time, space, cause, sequence: it was, again in Auerbach's vocabulary, horizontal.

Horace's rules also had some currency in the Middle Ages – at least enough to give a late production like Chaucer's *Troilus and Criseyde* the form of a perfectly plotted five-act structure – but they too were resuscitated with the rise of the vernacular, secular literatures in the fifteenth and sixteenth centuries. And in the meantime, plotting had received an infusion from that great goddess, Fortuna, whose wheel was not rectilinear (Aristotle's simple plot) or like two sides of an equilateral triangle (Aristotle's complex plot, peaking between complication and denouement) but circular and in constant movement in a post-lapsarian world. Thus Troilus' action is doubled from 'wo to wele, And after oute of joye', and the Renaissance, in spite of Aristotelian revivals, does not forget that perpetual turning. Edmund in *King Lear*, dying, knows that 'the wheel has come full circle, I am here'; and Marlowe, especially in *Edward II*, allows the revolution of several circles before the calamity, thus defying Aristotle's injunctions against episodic or epic styles in tragedy with stunning success.

Nevertheless, the medieval period is a kind of hiatus, and it is at that moment when Aristotle's *Poetics* was transmitted to western Europe by Averroës and Hermannus (translated into Latin by Hermannus in the thirteenth century, published in Venice in 1481, reprinted in 1515), that plot again took a central place in the creative theory of literature. A peculiar confluence of the humanist's need to outline the process of literature, with the reception of Averroës' commentary on a garbled version of the *Poetics*, created an epidemic of theory which is meticulously surveyed in Bernard Weinberg's two-volume work, *A History of Literary Criticism in the Italian Renaissance*. The result is infinite, unresolved disputation, coupled with the emergence of new rules to cover any exigency. The Cinquecento received a bastardized text which was gradually clarified, but was then, through over-interpretation, metamorphosed into a new thing through marriage with Horace, references to Plato, new formulations, and new literature.

The vernacular literatures were in need of an inclusive poetic, and seem to have been caught between their excitement at the ready-made format of Aristotle-cum-Horace and their nervousness at the shape of literature to come. The issue for them is indeed a renascence, in that they felt that the new vernacular compositions must revive the forms of classical literature in both plot and diction. They must show their equality to the classical period by adopting and applying classical criteria precisely. Antonio Riccoboni's late *De poetica Aristoteles cum Horatio collatus* (1592? – Weinberg's dating) is typical in that it draws parallels between Aristotle and Horace and is decorated with the rhetorical expansions which Horace's *Ars Poetica* invites. Even more interesting than the typical, probably, is the extreme and fussy example, as in the case of Castelvetro who, although rebelling, tried to be so thorough in the idea of imitation that he argued that the audience must be convinced that they are seeing not a representation, but the action itself, on the assumption, we may suppose, that a hero

will agree to schedule the circumstances of his life and tr
at seven o'clock on a given evening.

The difficulty lies, as mentioned previously, in the very real
to interpret Aristotle. The style of the *Poetics* is dismayingly
authoritative, but it is not an applied art, and the very idea of
application raises many questions and problems. It is, for example,
generally accepted that Avervoës garbled and confused the
Poetics as he 'arabized' it – that is, as he used Arab literature to
illustrate Aristotle's precepts. This is probably untrue, and a
Greco-Arabic scholar may one day be able to uncover the nature
and method of the 'garbling', showing the alterations necessary
when the theory is applied in a widespread and practical way. A
convenient exercise in illustrating the extent of the problems and
quarrels which the Italian theorists were later to turn up can be
taken by checking the quantity of entries under key Aristotelian
phrases in Weinberg's index. Like Averroës, the Italians were
locking horns with the problems of applying what looks like a
tidy theory to an entire literature.

Rather than tracing their struggles, a task competently handled
by Weinberg, let us turn back to the thorns in the Aristotelian
text itself, and to a much lesser extent to those of Horace and Plato.
The practitioner of Aristotle's art finds difficulty at almost every
turn and must finally act on his own interpretation. Because that
practitioner would be in process, it is with this aspect of Aristotle's
instructions that his troubles must begin. If he is to keep the scene
he is writing constantly before his eyes in order to maintain
verisimilitude, that scene must have a prior existence in history,
legend or experience. What then is the nature of invention? Is the
poet creating *ex nihilo* an action which will appear possible or prob-
able, or must he stick to the known? If he is to begin with a
general outline and then fill in particular episodes, could it perhaps
be that he is tied to a traditional story for the general and free in
the particular episodes? Or is he free in both? The literature

which Aristotle surveys is of little help in answering, because it is either lost or overwhelmingly traditional in subject.

The nature and placing of the crisis, between knitting and un-ravelling, has already been mentioned, but Aristotle complicates it. He mentions that in the *Lynceus* by Theodectes, the complication happened before the play proper, and therefore seems to imply that a play could, within the bounds of regularity, consist almost entirely of catastrophe or unravelling. In significant ways this would deny the idea of structuring in terms of a beginning, a middle and an end, if only because to change from this tripartite arrangement to the two norms of complication and catastrophe would logically imply breaking the play in the middle of the middle – especially if one wanted tidy and invariable rules. This kind of thinking is still current among, for example, some critics of Shakespeare who look for the crisis or turn as close as possible to Act III, Scene iii, and unfold meaning backward and forward from that point. And, of course, it was compositionally true in the structures of the great 'rules' plays of Corneille and Racine.

In his original description of tragedy, Aristotle claimed that every tragedy was made up of plot, character, diction, thought, spectacle, and song, of which plot was the most important. He also pointed out, however, that thought and character are the agents which naturally produced the success or failure of action. He seems to be saying that thought and character are efficient causes of action, a condition which binds the three as inseparable, not as separate constituents of the whole. Does he intend unity or division here? If plot is to be thought of as major, should not the action of character and of thought be included to bolster the slender idea of action as physical gesture? R. S. Crane in his classic essay, 'The Concept of Plot and the Plot of *Tom Jones*', presents a division of sorts which would leap over this problem. He claims that plot is a synthetic word and has three causal modifications, producing plots of action, plots of character, and plots of thought.

This interpretation would reject the plot of action as a mechanical arrangement alone, the conclusion reached through the careful rules and their exegesis which, by the seventeenth century, had reduced Aristotle's ideas to rigid and discardable conventions:

> It is impossible . . . to state adequately what any plot is unless we include in our formula all three of the elements or causes of which plot is the synthesis; and it follows also that plots will differ in structure according as one or another of the three causal ingredients is employed as the synthesizing principle. There are, thus, plots of action, plots of character, and plots of thought. In the first, the synthesizing principle is a completed change, gradual or sudden, in the situation of the protagonist, determined and effected by character and thought (as in *Oedipus* and *The Brothers Karamazov*); in the second, the principle is a completed process of change in the moral character of the protagonist, precipitated or molded by action, and made manifest both in it and in thought and feeling (as in James's *The Portrait of a Lady*); in the third, the principle is a completed process of change in the thought of the protagonist and consequently in his feelings, conditioned and directed by character and action (as in Pater's *Marius the Epicurean*).
>
> (Crane, p. 306)

This is an interesting perversion of Aristotle, using a far-reaching idea of plot and action to set up formal ideas palatable to the modern audience. Crane replaces the word tragedy with plot, and works from there. In section 18 of the *Poetics*, Aristotle had further complicated matters by mentioning four kinds of tragedy which would, ideally, be synthesized: complex tragedy (which depends on reversal or discovery and compares with Crane's plot of action), tragedy of suffering, tragedy of character, and spectacular tragedy. Crane makes the same kind of distinction, at the same time as he refers back to the earlier relationship of plot, character and thought, but he is ultimately submitting his own theory – a necessity which arises from the problematical nature of Aristotle's text.

Two other points in the *Poetics* need some mention – the idea of a single action, and the means of producing pity and fear. In literary theory after the *Poetics*, the use of a single action and the unity which springs from it received wide-spread attention, and led to the rule of the three unities – of action, time, and place. Aristotle went so far as to say that Homer was divinely inspired in that he selected one action for the fable of both the *Iliad* and the *Odyssey*, and did not make the mistake of trying to write about the whole Trojan war or every exploit of Ulysses. In order for plot to be effective, it must be whole – that is, have a beginning, middle and end, and have magnitude, a sense of size and ampleness which can be easily seized by the mind. Episodic structures deny this and lead to confusion, obscuring the end the poet has in mind. Aristotle does not care for double plots, but feels that amplitude is helped by a complex plot which uses recognition and reversal.

This stress on one whole action with episodes and redundancies pared away is not in itself conducive to theoretical wrangling. But action takes place in space and time, and very easily becomes involved in the root definition of *mimesis*. What is the relationship between the natural world and art? As all aestheticians know, this is an awesome question. Does Aristotle mean by *mimesis* that art imitates nature perfectly? If so, a tragedy enacted on the stage should convince us that it happens there, in one place which the stage mimetically represents and at one time, so that the action can be contained by the norms of temporal verisimilitude. Aristotle is off-hand about this, saying that the length depends on whatever time probably or necessarily is taken to accomplish a change from happiness to wretchedness or the reverse. The Italian and neo-classical critics generally opted for the three unities in drama, but with a few notable exceptions (dare one, in the company of such as Corneille and Ben Jonson, mention the apostate Anthony Munday, once 'our best at plotting'?), the best practising dramatists did not.

Lastly, how does a writer plot so as to create pity and fear not only during the performance of the drama, but when some one hears the tale? The most inessential part of the answer is explained in a straightforward way: pity and fear are often fairly easily aroused through skilful reversal or recognition, because surprise is added to logic. Unfortunately, pity and fear are not mechanical, and they join forces with the puzzling element of *je ne sais quoi* in Aristotle's exposition. Like action and plot, they are the end aimed at in tragedy, whatever this might mean. They rise naturally out of the action and are hence integral to plot. E. M. Forster, so anti-Aristotelian in intention, criticized Hardy's plots because they are too much controlled by a destiny above and beyond the action, whereas they should have an interior working out. Forster would stress the character of the protagonist working through action, but in all essentials he is asking for the same object in *mimesis* as Aristotle does.

R. S. Crane, in grappling with the problem, concludes that there is a difference between the structure of plot and its form ('working or power') which causes pity and fear and their catharsis:

> But this power, which constitutes the form of the plot, is obviously, from an artistic point of view, the most important virtue any drama or novel can have; it is that, indeed, which most sharply distinguishes works of imitation from all other kinds of literary productions. It follows, consequently, that the plot, considered formally of any imitative work is, in relation to the work as a whole, not simply a means – a 'framework' or 'mere mechanism' – but rather the final end which everything in the work, if that is to be felt as a whole, must be made, directly, or indirectly to serve. For the critic, therefore, the form of the plot is a first principle, which he must grasp as clearly as possible for any work he proposes to examine before he can deal adequately with the questions raised by its parts.
> (p. 308)

Again, this is a good, creative answer, with at least an Aristotelian tone.

Both Horace and Plato must receive much shorter shrift, for although their influence is very strong in the formation of neo-classical rules, they tend to be attached, in plot theory at least, to the larger and more explicit ideas of Aristotle. Many of Horace's theories are easily meshed with Aristotle's, although two of his ideas – of decorum and the task of art to teach and entertain (*docere*, *delectare*) – have a life of their own. Decorum demands that all parts of the work fit together not only according to veri-similitude, although this is very important to his theory, but also according to internal rules which establish their fitness. In no way is Horace interested in a grotesque which goes beyond decorum, for he opens his *Epistola ad Pisones*, the original title of the *Ars Poetica*, with a risible image of human heads and horses' necks, feathered animals and fish-bottomed women, which only an absurd painter could possibly figure forth:

> Humano capiti cervicem pictor equinam
> Iungere si velit, & varias inducers plumas,
> Undique collatis membris: ut turpiter atrum
> Desinat in piscem mulier formosa superne:
> Spectatum admissi risum teneatis amici?

He is acutely aware of the audience which must be persuaded toward the lessons art teaches by a mimetic approach which reflects the world as it is and can be ordered according to the invention of the poet. Genres must be carefully considered in relationship to the decorous style pre-ordained for them, and human manners and customs studied and properly represented in art – old men must seem like old men, and young men like young. If everything is properly ordered, the genre maintained, and language in orderly control, then pleasure will arise, and through it the poet will exert his duty to teach. Poetry thus takes on a moral function which may have lain behind the ethical philosophy of Aristotle but is not especially evident in his *Poetics*.

When Aristotle married Horace in the Cinquecento, this became a major unitive issue.

It was both aided and hindered by Platonic additions. Although Plato praised the inspiration of poetry in the *Phaedrus* and *Ion*, the only significant document for our purposes is a small section of Book X of the *Republic*, where he placed *mimesis* third, after reality and the shadow of reality, and banished poets from the state because they did not tell the truth. This led inevitably to questions about the nature of *mimesis*, not only in respect to the connection between art and the real, but in terms of its *raison d'être* in a Christian world. Rather weary Cinquecento statements that it is all right because it is useful are not enough. Is *mimesis* in any way true, can *mimesis* and ontology lie down together? Shakespeare built an aesthetic metaphor out of the question:

AUDREY I do not know what 'poetical' is: is it honest in deed and word? is it a true thing?

TOUCHSTONE No, truly; for the truest poetry is the most feigning; and lovers are given to poetry, and what they swear in poetry it may be said as lovers they do feign.

AUDREY Do you wish then that the gods had made me poetical?

TOUCHSTONE I do, truly; for thou swearest to me thou art honest; now, if thou wert a poet, I might have some hope thou didst feign.

AUDREY Would you not have me honest?

TOUCHSTONE No, truly, unless thou wert hard-favoured; for honesty coupled to beauty is to have honey a sauce to sugar.

JAQUES (*aside*) A material fool!

(*As You Like It*, III, iii)

Never has the question been better or more succinctly answered – honesty and art, honey and sugar, and the insouciant shrug of the fool. It has, nevertheless, become the lasting irritation. In what way is fiction real, and does the very fact that it is selectively plotted and arranged move *mimesis* from truth to lies?

By the seventeenth century the rules were established and a

literature of rules in progress, but there was no possibility of triumph or real majority. No sooner did it become commonplace to talk about the rules than the rebels made themselves heard. What became known as the Battle of the Ancients and Moderns was fought on many fronts in a period leading to the schismatic transitions of the eighteenth century. An inclusive document summarizing most of the quarrels and issues is Dryden's technically elegant *Essay of Dramatic Poesy*. To the far-off accompaniment of cannons as the Dutch and English engage in sea-battle, four points of view garbed in Greek names – Eugenius, Crites, Lisideius, Neander – float up the quiet Thames. The subject is plot and rhetoric, and the arguments deal with regularity as opposed to irregularity, the superiority of the Ancients or Moderns, the French or English dramatists, or, quintessentially, how to compose and what kind of composition to praise. It is a fair four-way discussion and is significantly unresolved. It has generally been assumed that Neander is Dryden, and certainly in his 'Defence of an Essay of Dramatic Poesy' he speaks *in propria persona*, but the calm embracing of manifold viewpoints in the original essay, the friendly intermingling, and the calm irresolution are much more telling as an interim stance. The battle moves from this relative latitudinarianism to viciousness in the next century as classical tenure relaxes and the shadow of the Goddess Dullness darkens the once enlightening and orderly rules of literary excellence.

It would be wrong to think that the conventions of plotting died when *Tristram Shandy* illustrated their utter impossibility:

> My mother, you must know, – but I have fifty things more necessary to let you know first, – I have a hundred difficulties which I have promised to clear up, and a thousand distresses and domestic misadventures crouding in upon me thick and three-fold, one upon the neck of another, – a cow broke in (to-morrow morning) to my uncle *Toby's* fortifications, and eat up two ratios and half of dried grass, tearing up the sods with it, which faced his horn-work and

covered way. – *Trim* insists upon being tried by a court-martial, – the cow to be shot, – *Slop* to be *crucifix'd*, – myself to be *tristram'd*, and at my very baptism made a martyr of; – poor unhappy devils that we all are! – I want swaddling, – but there is no time to be lost in exclamations. – I have left my father lying across his bed, and my uncle *Toby* in his old fringed chair, sitting beside him, and promised I would go back to them in half an hour, and five and thirty minutes are laps'd already. – Of all the perplexities a mortal author was ever seen in, – this certainly is the greatest, – for I have *Hafen Slawken-bergius's* folio, Sir, to finish – a dialogue between my father and my uncle Toby, upon the solution of *Prignitz*, *Scroderus*, *Ambrose Paraeus*, *Ponocrates* and *Grangousier* to relate, – a tale out of *Slawken-bergius* to translate, and all this in five minutes less, than no time at all; – such a head! – would to heaven! my enemies only saw the inside of it!

Conventions die hard, and even overt denials help to keep them alive, but theory has the habit of resurrection.

One of the most influential critics of the mid-twentieth century, Northrop Frye, has revived Aristotle and re-interpreted him with a strong Jungian bias. Although Frye's *Anatomy of Criticism* spills Aristotle's nouns almost randomly, the most noticeable aspect of the book is its separation from the past and, above all, the curious quasi-Jungian developments of the word 'myth' and the way that this idea is connected to Aristotle's *mythos* or plot. That Frye is interested in plots cannot be doubted, but all of the Aristotelian paraphernalia are clearly little more than notes towards the very different development of the concept of myth in litera-ture. Of his four theoretical essays, 'Theory of Myths' is dominant. It is longer than his 'Theory of Genres' and completely eclipses both 'Theory of Modes' and 'Theory of Symbols'. As a theore-tician, Frye instantly reveals his initial dependence on Aristotle and derives much of his vocabulary from him, but he quickly shoots from him to his own creation. It would perhaps be convenient to rank Frye as the Horace *de nos jours* – witty, not entirely independent of his sources, eclectic, descriptive, and authoritarian.

His ambition is to describe and evaluate literature: in many ways his book reads like a latter-day defence of poetry against the encroaching enemy, and indeed his 'Polemical Introduction' makes a special plea for criticism as a systematic study. The natural sciences are justified by the body of empirical nature behind them, and so literature must be shown to have its palpable corps from which can be drawn important systems and systematic analyses. This introduction falls into the category of pseudo-science, but one cannot help wondering whether the scientist is really eager to see this kind of methodological toadying from the humanist. Calling on Aristotle gives Frye venerable authority and reproduces with serious modern clarity the medieval technique once parodied by Pertelote.

He begins with the beginning of Aristotle, and within a page and a half of his first essay, 'Historical Criticism: Theory of Modes', has ejected his reader from Aristotelianism to the highly original Fryean theoretical hypothesis. While Aristotle was setting up the logistics of his essay, he remarked that literature presents men who are better or worse or the same as we ourselves are. From this unprepossessing statement, Frye constructs the ground-work of his system – and in an instant gives a schematized method for viewing all kinds of plotting. The entire section is quoted as a means of conveying both his theoretical accomplish-ment and the creative excitement which he has infused into his work:

> Fictions, therefore may be classified, not morally, but by the hero's power of action, which may be greater than ours, less, or roughly the same. Thus:
>
> 1. If superior in *kind* both to other men and to the environment of other men, the hero is a divine being, and the story about him will be a *myth* in the common sense of a story about a god. Such stories

have an important place in literature, but are as a rule found outside the normal literary categories.

2. If superior in *degree* to other men and to his environment, the hero is the typical hero of *romance*, whose actions are marvellous but who is himself identified as a human being. . . . Here we have moved from myth, properly so called, into legend, folk tale, *märchen*, and their literary affiliates and derivatives.

3. If superior in degree to other men but not to his natural environment, the hero is a leader. . . . This is the hero of the *high mimetic* mode, of most epic and tragedy, and is primarily the kind of hero that Aristotle had in mind.

4. If superior neither to other men nor to his environment, the hero is one of us: we respond to a sense of his common humanity, and demand from the poet the same canons of probability that we find in our own experience. This gives us the hero of the *low mimetic* mode, of most comedy and of realistic fiction. 'High' and 'low' have no connotations of comparative value, but are purely diagrammatic. . . .

5. If inferior in power of intelligence to ourselves, so that we have the sense of looking down on a scene of bondage, frustration, or absurdity, the hero belongs to the *ironic* mode. . . .

Looking over this table, we can see that European fiction, during the last fifteen centuries, has steadily moved its center of gravity down the list.

(pp. 33–34)

By the inclusion of 'high mimetic', 'low mimetic', and 'ironic' modes, Frye has telescoped the whole neo-classical problem of genres and styles, and in the categorical arrangement presented an unnervingly thorough scheme for classifying all plots by examining their heroes.

His systematizing goes further as it mingles with vegetation cycles, sun gods and other Jungian mythic concepts, but there is frequent recurrence of the Aristotelian vocabulary and progressive redefinition of central Greek terms. Just as the history of literature is the march of the theory of modes, so Frye conceives of a constant shifting and revaluation of Aristotle's words with the history of literature. For example, he takes Aristotle's 'thought' (*dianoia* – he insists on the Greek word, apparently because he feels it needs constant retranslation), and claims that the modern critical term is 'theme', that which answers the question 'What's the *point* of this story?' (p. 52). In his later essay, 'Myth, Fiction and Displacement', he carries his vocabulary development into new areas. He claims here that theme is threefold – that it is 'subject' in the conventional sense, that it is *dianoia* or '[the] sententious reflexion that the poem suggests to the meditative reader', and that it is beyond our primitive literary vocabulary and has a third sense as 'the *mythos* or plot examined as a simultaneous unity, when the entire shape of it is clear in our minds' (p. 24). Theme, then, becomes the universal word, replacing plot or, as he will later uneasily indicate, mingling closely with it in the production of action (p. 28).

The book from which this latter essay is taken, *Fables of Identity*, deals with practical critical application of the theory Frye undertook in *Anatomy of Criticism*. This transfer creates the same kind of dispersal and confusion of critical terms which characterized the attempts to work from Aristotle's theory to practice at a much earlier period in what Frye would like to hear called the science of literature. There can be no doubt that the key factor in literary criticism deals with the misfortune that our critical vocabulary is primitive and that we simply do not have the words to deliver the concise intellection we can achieve. It is equally true that words are subject to mutation in time, so that *mythos* and *dianoia* should, in the natural order of things, take on new meaning. What is not entirely clear is Frye's reason for clinging persistently to Greek words which he must splice or disjoin, equate or rob of connotation, according to the stress of the moment of criticism. Frye is one of our greatest critics, and one cannot help wishing that his examination of form and content (*mythos* and myth) had clarified the critical vocabulary rather more.

In 1928, Edwin Muir published a small volume whose subject was generally the novel as dealt with previously by Forster, Lubbock and Carruthers, and specifically the kinds of plot ordering which go into its various structures. The book, *Structure of the Novel*, is both unpretentious and important as an introductory study. In 1967, it went into its tenth impression and still maintains a market and currency. One of the habits of narrative criticism in the twentieth century has been its concentration on the novel to the exclusion of most other forms, and Muir's essay is within this mainstream. As it was written before the avant-garde chiliastic movements, it has that uncluttered naïveté which now marks most criticism which has not borrowed greatly from psychology or philosophy or both. Like most descriptive books, it is diagrammatic, and is particularly notable for its direct classifications and purely literary concerns. For any one wishing to start with the novel and having a residual belief that Aristotle might have been right when he said the plot was the soul of fiction, this apparently simple book has its value. It also contributes another chapter in the history of the complex problem of what a plot actually is and how it can be described.

'The term plot . . . is a definite term, it is a literary term, and it is universally applicable. It can be used in the widest popular sense. It designates for everyone, not merely for the critic, the chain of events in a story and the principle which knits it together' (p. 16). This is a convenient reiteration of our primal ideas about plot, and the early chapters on the novels of action and character are clear: the novel of action creates limited characters to bolster event and includes most adventure stories and works of a purely episodic nature, such as Marlowe's *Doctor Faustus*. The novel of character (like *Vanity Fair*) cares very little for the causal development of action and is plotted haphazardly so that its entire energy can be concentrated on the ample description of characters. In his later chapter on time and space (in which there is no metaphysical tomfoolery, something quite alien to Muir's vision) he points out that the novel of action depends on its unfolding in time and cares little about the geography of space, whereas the novel of character depends on space and is primarily atemporal.

Aside from his classifications and the initial instructions they convey, the major chapter is on the dramatic novel, which is the perfection of style and corresponds to what Aristotle would have described as tragedy – although Muir eschews any mention of Aristotle. In the dramatic novel (first written by Jane Austen, continued through *Wuthering Heights* to some of Hardy) time and character are equally important and do not encroach on each other – in fact, they are blurred under the dynamics of the life-giving force in the interior workings of the fiction. Muir quotes Nietzsche's idea of the 'erosion of contours' and says that 'the lines of action must be laid down, but life must perpetually flood them, bend them . . .' (p. 48). He is chiefly concerned to say that in the dramatic novel there is no imbalance which would allow stress in any direction, that the plot is not obtrusive in its action nor is the depiction of character, and that the novelist, while plotting, never errs. Charlotte Brontë almost made it, except for the inconsistency of burning to death the first Mrs Rochester which belies the integrity of the work and describes the difference between success and failure.

What is most interesting about Muir's thesis is his language when he is talking about the most important form of the novel. Every part of the plot dovetails perfectly in the dramatic novel and a supernal tone is achieved, but Muir's thinking becomes fuzzy as he describes it and is released only in the next chapter on space and time when he can talk about the tragic shadow of time in *Wuthering Heights*. Like Aristotle, he is at root dependent on a *je ne sais quoi* for the soul of the perfectly plotted work, and aside from talking about bending and erosion, the tight, direct vocabulary he had set up is inadequate. Moreover, behind his arguments is subjective choice – *Wuthering Heights*, for example, has not always or even frequently before our period been considered a great and certainly not a unified novel, and his defence at this crucial point becomes sub-verbal, emotional and analytical in only a very limited way. Unlike Frye, Muir did not try to create an expansive literary aesthetic, depending rather on simpler words within the traditional vocabulary, like unadorned plot. He alone in the twentieth century seemed to feel that it could stand great weight without alteration and development, but he has only partly succeeded in proving it, even within his narrow scope.

In concluding this section on plot and *mimesis*, let us turn briefly to the theories of Leo Tolstoi, a profoundly mimetic writer who, without written recourse to Aristotle, echoes in nineteenth-century dress the theories and relationships which keep *mimesis* alive. In his Second Epilogue to *War and Peace* (ed. George Gibian, New York, 1966), he argues as Aristotle once did of the superiority of literature to history. Sir Philip Sidney had gone one further in the sixteenth century, claiming literature to be above both history and philosophy, and this is in fact much closer to Tolstoi's position. Because *War and Peace* is a novel about the Napoleonic invasion of Russia and the whole Napoleonic era, Tolstoi sees it as the deepest and most passionate expression of history, but spiritualized, personalized history with the specifics of individual lives attached to it. At the nexus of the novel's idea is the concurrence too of manifold philosophical and theological ideas which the action plays out and which, initially, produced both the action and the characters who inhabit that action. This is art in the midst of all of its highest ambitions, close to a Wagnerian multifarious achievement of both conscious and unconscious. In the Second Epilogue, Tolstoi is angry at the failure of history to invent new conceptions although it has rejected those of the ancients. Because history has failed, he claims for his novel the seat that history had once had. This he feels he can do because of his adherence to historical detail and because of his humanizing and spiritualizing of the whole by the creation of characters who flow realistically through the historical conflagration.

This is *mimesis* of the most radical sort, for in it everything, from real accounts of battles to fictive characters, is seen as a reflection of nature, life as it is lived and can be logically understood. In all of Tolstoi's thought, whatever breaks faith with nature is culpable; it is beyond the intense morality which is art, and is pejoratively absurd. Shakespeare's plays fall into this latter category, and Tolstoi's criticism of them, particularly of *King Lear*, is one of the most curious and exciting documents in the long struggle of *mimesis* against metaphoric interpretations of reality.

Tolstoi's life was haunted by the chasm separating his dislike of Shakespeare from the universal adulation which even great aesthetes like Turgenev shared, and at the age of seventy-five he once again set for himself the task of reading through all of Shakespeare objectively to see if he might, after all, have been wrong. His conclusions are astonishing but well supported: as an artist and hence transmitter of nature, Shakespeare is immoral and a charlatan:

> From his first words, exaggeration is seen: the exaggeration of events, the exaggeration of emotion, and the exaggeration of effects. One sees at once that he does not believe in what he says, that it is of no necessity to him, that he invents the events he describes and is indifferent to his characters — that he has conceived them only for the stage and therefore makes them do and say only what may strike his public, and so we do not believe either in the events or in the actions or in the sufferings of the characters. Nothing demonstrates so clearly the complete absence of aesthetic feeling in Shakespeare as comparison between him and Homer. The works which we call the works of Homer are artistic, poetic, original works, lived through by the author or authors; whereas the works of Shakespeare — borrowed as they are and externally, like mosaics, artificially fitted

together piecemeal from bits invented for the occasion – have nothing whatever in common with art and poetry.

(p. 55)

What is most wrong with Shakespeare is that he was a plagiarist and wantonly stole the outlines of his plots from writers superior to himself. In every instance, he ruined his source by neglecting causality, motivation, and verisimilitude: thus Cinthio's tale is better and more socially decorous than *Othello* and the early play *King Leir and His Daughters* more true to nature and human action than Shakespeare's adaptation.

To prove his point in detail, Tolstoi goes through *King Lear* scene by scene, and most convincingly shows that people do not act like this in real human situations, nor are any of their speeches truly reflected mimetically in Shakespeare's poetry. The words of the curses and the fool's metaphors are not intrinsic to the language of passion: reality is not like this, and art is an imitation of reality.

> However absurd it [*King Lear*] may appear in my rendering (which I have endeavoured to make as impartial as possible), I may confidently say that in the original it is yet more absurd. For any man of our time – if he were not under the hypnotic suggestion that this drama is the height of perfection – it would be enough to read it to its end (had he sufficient patience for this) to be convinced that far from its being the height of perfection, it is a very bad, carelessly composed production, which, if it could have been of interest to a certain public at a certain time, cannot evoke among us anything but aversion and weariness.
>
> (p. 34)

In Tolstoi's view it is an act of immorality to perpetuate the myth of Shakespeare's greatness when moral writing which reflects man's life and spirit in history is in existence and furnishes man's true accomplishment in art.

Tolstoi is advocating the *mimesis* of realism, but aggrandized by a metaphysical view of the world and action in it. In no way can his objections to Shakespeare's plot be honestly answered. The first few scenes of *King Lear* are mind-bogglingly irrelevant as a mimetic pattern, and defences of the play must take either the metaphoric or archetypal route. It is perfectly clear that Shakespeare is using plot not as a figuring forth of action which could logically or possibly occur in history. Perhaps he is dealing with the inner plotting of the *psychomachia*, for if he wished to deal with causality and was genuinely dependent on his source play, he would have found ample motivation ready-made for him. Whatever the answer, we find plot turning on a dimension whose apparent coin is action but in which the abiding mimetic conventions of verisimilitude are firmly flouted. Tolstoi belongs to the older and more logically comprehensible tradition, and would doubtless have found Augustine's defence of metaphor in the *De Doctrina Christiana* as outrageously unnatural as he found the plot and language of Shakespeare's plays.

The fatal attraction of Aristotelian *mimesis* lies behind most of the theories which have been developed about literature. Very often the idea of the morality of truth has been uppermost because of the human hunger and thirst after knowledge which would produce an ontological fiction of the sort which creates Tolstoi's moral-aesthetic universe, a universe in which art asserts its power to imitate nature exactly and helps the reader to comprehend the spiritual pattern behind existence. The dark side of this high expectation from the fictive cosmos is the sober, ultimately Platonic acceptance that the fictions which we so remorsely love share the plight of love itself when, as our supreme fiction, it faces reality without the transformations of art:

ORLANDO Then in mine own person I die.

ROSALIND No, faith, die by attorney. The poor world is almost six thousand years old, and in all this time there was not any man died in his own person, videlicet, in a love-cause. Troilus had his brains dashed out with a Grecian club; yet he did what he could to die before, and he is one of the patterns of love. Leander, he would have lived for many a fair year, though Hero had turned nun, if it had not been for a hot midsummer night; for, good youth, he went but forth to wash him in the Hellespont and being taken with the cramp was drowned: and the foolish chroniclers of that age found it was 'Hero of Sestos'. But these are all lies: men have died from time to time and worms have eaten them, but not for love.

(*As You Like It*, IV i)

3
The Struggle to Replace Plot:
Poiesis and Time

Because we are no longer comfortable with the inherited idea of plot, we are the more likely to agree with Henry James that the house of fiction has a million windows, and modern critics of the novel have attempted to open many of them. In the last twenty years, as the New Criticism became very old and the neo-Aristotelianism of the Chicago School waned, the novel maintained its replacement of the poem as the dominant subject of a criticism which is both descriptive and creative. All of its critics are theoreticians: even the artist, when he turns to criticism, leaves the moment of practical achievement behind him. Frank Kermode, commenting on Iris Murdoch's criticism, illustrated the bedevilling split between literature and thinking about literature:

> Here [in the dissidence between the inherited form and our own reality] I have in mind Iris Murdoch, a writer whose persistent and radical thinking about the form has not as yet been fully reflected in her own fiction. . . . When Miss Murdoch herself succeeds in writing a novel which contains opaque, impenetrable persons in a form which nowhere betrays a collapse from the strict charities of the imagination into the indulgent mythologies of fantasy, we shall have more evidence that the history of the novel is a history of anti-novels.

> (pp. 130–1)

The major contemporary direction in thinking about the novel as the dominant narrative form in the last few hundred years has been towards a description of process, of how the writer succeeds in conveying a meaning through narration. In strictest definition, it is necessary to say that critics are thinking of the constituents of plot. Malcolm Bradbury, in his article on an approach through structure, claims that we must think of the narration and structure not in generalities, but in terms of the composition sentence by sentence – in other words, how the very action of the verbal arrangement is plotted. However the various vocabularies are arranged, it is quite clear that the subject of interest is the construction which produces the desired effect, a way of talking about the informing movement of idea and meaning in the novel, and the means by which that motion is accomplished through the narrating voice.

The bibliography lists several critics who talk well and creatively about these aspects of the novel; all of them could be said to be interested in the root nature of plot but have substituted other words to broaden and deepen what that word might imply. As a matter of convenience their achievements can be summarized under the word *poiesis*, a rather artificial term indicating the lyrical and creative innovations which their theories superimpose on the idea of plot. These critics can be seen as differentiated from those theorizers who reflect the strong currents of contemporary chiliastic philosophy or anthropology and whose preoccupation with movement and progress within the work of literature centres on time – what Aristotle in a very rudimentary way described as beginning, middle, and end.

Before turning to *poiesis*, however, we ought to give at least momentary attention to an important book which stands outside of these rather arbitrary categories – *The Nature of Narrative* by Robert Scholes and Robert Kellogg. The individual chapter on plot is not very enlightening in that it limits itself to cyclic, anthropological thinking and is highly reliant on Mircea Eliade and F. M. Cornford. What is of particular interest is the categories into which the authors divide all narration. These categories, like the substance of the entire book, are not drawn specifically from the novel, but from a large and inclusive view of the sum of narrative western literature. The two over-all and antithetical divisions are *empirical* and *fictional*, and both struggle against what Aristotle had to say about *mythos*: the system is, therefore, an attempt to trample on the head of the serpent and talk about free human creativity beyond hide-bound *mimesis*. This is how they describe and subdivide their categories:

Empirical narrative replaces allegiance to the *mythos* with allegiance to reality. We can subdivide the impulse toward empirical narrative into two main components: the *historical* and the *mimetic*. The historical component owes its allegiance specifically to truth of fact and to the actual past rather than to a traditional version of the past. It requires for its development means of accurate measurement in time and space, and concepts of causality referable to human and natural rather than to supernatural agencies. . . . The mimetic component owes its allegiance not to truth of fact but to truth of sensation and environment, depending on observation of the present rather than investigation of the past. It requires for its development socio-logical and psychological concepts of behaviour and mental process, . . . Mimetic narrative is the antithesis of mythic in that it tends toward plotlessness. Its ultimate form is the 'slice of life'. Biography and autobiography are both empirical forms of narrative. In biography, which is developed first, the historical impulse dominates; in autobiography, the mimetic.

The *fictional* branch of narrative replaces allegiance to the *mythos* with allegiance to the ideal. We can subdivide the impulse toward fictional narrative into two main components also: the *romantic* and the *didactic*. The writer of fiction is set free from the bonds of tradition and the bonds of empiricism as well. His eye is not on the external world but on the audience, which he hopes to delight or instruct, giving it either what it wants or what he thinks it needs.

(pp. 13–14)

There is much here which is new and an infinite deal which is controversial, but the ideas must be considered, if only because this categorical arrangement virtually denies *mythos* as a way of talking about literature in its relationship to either the real or the ideal.

POIESIS

Poiesis retains a preoccupation with the movement and organization of the primary *mythos*, but is indifferent to the stress of mechanical plotting. Peter K. Garrett in his book *Scene and Symbol from George Eliot to James Joyce* equates it with a search for the components and methodology of meaning, and understands it as both complete and beyond mechanics when he says '. . . I would not have that meaning misconceived as a paraphrasable thematic content which can be abstracted from form. All of a novel's elements, from its basic verbal unity to its composite units of character and event, ordered as the novel presents them, combine to produce its meaning' (p. 8). The stress of *poiesis* is multiform, but can probably be viewed with most clarity when it exists in the art form rather than in criticism.

In Joyce's *A Portrait of the Artist as a Young Man*, Stephen Dedalus struggles with an aesthetic of form which he calls the 'rhythm of beauty' and defines as 'the first formal esthetic relation of part to part in any esthetic whole or of an esthetic whole to its part or parts or of any part to the esthetic whole of which it is a part' (Penguin edition, Harmondsworth, 1968, p. 206). Working through and past Thomist vocabulary, he is finally able to articulate what the *poiesis* of form is:

Even in literature, the highest and most spiritual art, the forms are often confused. The lyrical form is in fact the simplest verbal gesture of an instant of emotion, a rhythmical cry such as ages ago cheered on the man who pulled at the oar or dragged stones up a slope. He who utters it is more conscious of the instant of emotion than of himself as feeling emotion. The simplest epical form is seen emerging out of lyrical literature when the artist prolongs and broods upon himself as the centre of an epical event and this form progresses till the centre of emotional gravity is equidistant from the artist himself and from others. The narrative is no longer purely personal. The personality of the artist passes into the narration itself, flowing round and round the persons and the action like a vital sea. This progress you will see easily in that old English ballad *Turpin Hero* which begins in the first person and ends in the third person. The dramatic form is reached when the vitality which has flowed and eddied round each person fills every person with such vital force that he or she assumes a proper and intangible esthetic life. The personality of the artist, at first a cry or a cadence or a mood and then a fluid and lambent narrative, finally refines itself out of existence, impersonalizes itself, so to speak. The esthetic image in the dramatic form is life purified in and projected from the human imagination. The mystery of esthetic, like that of material creation, is accomplished. The artist, like the God of creation, remains within or behind or beyond or above his handiwork, invisible, refined out of existence, indifferent, paring his fingernails.

(pp. 214–15)

Like Aristotle, Stephen Dedalus works his way through genres to the supremacy of the dramatic form, but he does so by stressing the artist in the act of creation, beginning with the lyric in which his personality is dominant and progressing to the finality of the dramatic from which he is able to withdraw and where he achieves godly status. The key idea has to do with the location of the artist's personality *vis-à-vis* the artistic product, and the relative distances which can be achieved between artist and work. This concentration on the thinking, creating mind of the artist is what must be understood as *poiesis* pressing forward towards meaning in the action of the literary piece. Because the artist is so utterly involved in the creation of genre and form through the infusion or separation of his personality, he is in constant relationship with that art, even if he is only paring his fingernails indifferently. *Poiesis* demands this shift from the completed work which consumed all of pre-Romantic attention to the process and the creating mind whose occupation Coleridge described in the words 'esem-plastic imagination'.

Joseph Conrad, in his Preface to the *Nigger of the Narcissus*, goes a step further to talk not only about the artist's presence in the work he has created, but of his passionate will to mould the reaction of the audience, 'to make you hear, to make you feel . . . before all, to make you see' (p. 162). In the writer's manipulation of form is the recurrent urge to force the reader to grasp what Dorothy Van Ghent called the world of the author's imagination, and to find the just means to comprehend that fiction. Prior definition is of little or no assistance in performing this creative act, and the spawning of vocabularies in the attempt to do it is inevitable.

Of these vocabularies, one of the most striking and historically apt is Ralph Freedman's introduction of the term 'lyrical novel'. Edith Wharton had an embryonic instinct of the same sort when she claimed that 'modern fiction really began when the "action" of the novel was transferred from the street to the soul' (by Mme de la Fayette in *La Princesse de Clèves*), but Freedman's idea is much larger. The lyrical novel is interior, it is not didactic or dramatic, and it is characterized by intensity and its approximation to poetic genres. It is significantly a symbolic form and lends itself to the kind of criticism and analysis we normally expend on poetry. Even picaresque and allegorical narratives can and do participate, in so far as they are 'lyrically conceived' – that is, as long as their stress is symbolic rather than mimetic. Although germinally this conception has much in common with the long current practice of transferring poetic vocabulary to the novel, Freedman, by expanding ideas inherent in German Roman-ticism, has done much to isolate a genre within the novelistic form.

His work is related to the controversial 'stream of consciousness' technique in which what is narrated is to be seen as a transcript of the mind as it goes through an inner articulation of experience. The French term *monologue intérieure* is more precise, for it implies a rationality and intelligence which 'stream of consciousness' cannot. Taken for granted in most casual uses of the term (which we apply to such structurally careful writers as Virginia Woolf and James Joyce in the early parts of *A Portrait* and in *Ulysses*) is the mobile will of the author shaping either a high or low *mimetic* consciousness – a Mrs Dalloway or a Benjie in *The Sound and the Fury*. In its root sense, however, as a term in which choice and artistic control cannot be exercised, it is far removed from this meaning. In *Stream of Consciousness in the Modern Novel*, Robert Humphrey sorts out its connotations and separates its false from its true types, beginning with its coining by William James as a phrase suitable for psychological study.

Despite this refining of the term, its popular usage will be continued as a descriptive term which has done much to enable the writer to narrate the action which has moved from the street to the soul. The rational mind has its own action, and this method of reproducing its rhythms and fragmentary association of ideas created still another branch of new literature within the over-all bourgeois notion of the novel. In its fluidity it can co-operate with older, more firmly established genres – as an extension of drama (the soliloquy is a pre-type) or in epic form, as Joyce proved in *Ulysses*. It is also deeply satisfying to that common modern desire to believe that psychological discoveries can be cemented to the symbol or image-making faculty of the mind. If the novel can show a unity between psyche, private symbol and the *poiesis* of art, the esemplastic imagination can list no greater achievement.

Gimmickry always, unfortunately, abounds whenever vocabularies are being created. When Alan Friedman in *The Turn of the Novel* creates a new modifying phrase for fiction, the 'stream of conscience', he is guilty of causing confusion with an idea whose conception is a good and original way of talking about the fascination of plot. He sees the events of a novel as transmitting the flux of imaged experience as characters are translated progressively from innocence to experience; as this happens, the novel in action creates an 'ethical form – that is, the stream of moral outcomes – a stream of conscience' (p. 16). Aware that his rather loosely expressed argument may cause difficulty, Friedman explains in a footnote the difference between 'stream of conscience' and 'stream of consciousness':

> Both 'streams' are metaphors and both refer to processes or currents in fiction, but there the parallel stops. Indeed, the flux or stream of conscience, insofar as it is designed as a term to include every mode by which the self responds to the world, would include the stream of consciousness as one such mode.
>
> The stream of consciousness is a technique (or a variety of such techniques) for rendering consciousness in fiction. The stream of conscience is not a technique. Whereas evidently novels can exist without rendering a stream of consciousness, no novel can exist without rendering a stream of conscience. The latter is the moral *movement* of fiction itself . . .; it is the evolution of the full moral complexity of a work of fiction, developed and elaborated as a process . . . through the structure of events. . . . The stream of events in a novel is the flux of experience viewed from the outside; an architectural view. The stream (or flux) of conscience is an inside view: it is the flux of experience viewed morally.
>
> (pp. 190–1)

Friedman, within his newly created terminology, sees an early twentieth century shift from moral completion within the literary form to moral openness, and in order to analyse this he borrows from Robert M. Adams (in *Strains of Discord*) the idea of open and closed ends in the novel. Once again there is cause for confusion. Adams is essentially talking about formal construction and about normative resolutions as opposed to the tendency towards open-endedness in the novel of process, whereas Friedman is concerned with the moral flux and whether it is contained or opened out into continuing experience as it is, for example, in D. H. Lawrence's *The Rainbow*. This vocabulary of open and closed novels is a straight substitution for the process-product antithesis instituted during the great eighteenth century change of taste and most completely illustrated by the formal mysteries of *Tristram Shandy* which may or may not be finished. In our century it has become obsessive not only as a critical and compositional problem, but as a metaphysic treating of our concept of time and our distrust of all the comforts and seductions of form.

In 1921, Percy Lubbock celebrated Henry James's excellence as a novelist by praising fiction which uses its narrator as the central and active intelligence – as, that is, the prime mover and controller of the *mythos* – an idea which Aristotle would find repugnant. This led inevitably to an explosion of essays on omniscient narrators, the absence or withdrawal of the narrator, the intrusive narrator, etc., footnoted by Norman Friedman in his 1955 *PMLA* article. Since that time there have been refinements and closer definitions by such critics as Wayne Booth, whose ideas about fiction go far beyond the stress on the place of the narrator, into close studies of modern rhetoric and how structure can be discovered in the details of the fictional form.

Allied to Booth's interests in many ways is the book of practical criticism by Mark Schorer, *The World We Imagine* (New York, 1969). Schorer's intention is to revive the primacy of technique:

Technique is really what T. S. Eliot means by 'convention': any selection, structure or distortion, any form or rhythm imposed upon the world of action; by means of which, it should be added, our apprehension of the world of action is enriched or renewed. In this sense, everything is technique which is not the lump of experience itself, and one cannot properly say that a writer has no technique, or that he eschews technique, for, being a writer, he cannot do so.

(p. 5)

From this statement, Schorer can go only to individual analysis, to uncovering the technical styles which create each fiction's world. The method is above rules and deeply concerned with fresh discovery of the content which can only be delivered by form.

Schorer and Booth have been singled out because they typify the critic who is committed to the detail of literary development. Simon O. Lesser's book, *Fiction and the Unconscious*, is tantalized by the action of narrative art for entirely different reasons, and sees the function of literature as threefold: to give pleasure (of a deep psychological sort), to avoid or relieve guilt and anxiety, and to facilitate perception (p. 125). Lesser is clearly Freudian, but, like most Freudians, he is very attached to the consolations of form and therefore of Aristotelianism. The plot with its perfected arrangement is a joy to the disturbed subconscious. Its ability to use each detail to effect the pattern of the whole action, which is causal in structure, pleases the reader whose mind is usually not adequately persistent to do this on its own. 'From the flux of experience [the artist] must abstract something which has beginning, middle and end' (p. 151). Form naturally creates clarity, and from this clarity is learned perceptions about forms of guilt and anxieties which we share with the fictive characters. This is probably not classifiable as *poiesis*, but it is another example of the independent developments which plot has achieved in contemporary criticism.

Finally, it is worth mentioning the new geometric forms which have been granted to various kinds of plot. The linear plot, the parallel lines of double plots, the circle, rising and falling action, are all very old and so, by now, is Tristram's jagged, looped, backtracking diagram, but the desire for new geometry is not exhausted.

E. M. Forster, who wanted at least to appear as though he were overturning apple-carts, begins with his version of 'story' – that aspect which makes the audience want to know what happens next, moves on to 'plot' which rises from 'story' and which is 'the novel in its logical intellectual aspect' (p. 92) and ends with 'pattern and rhythm'. The 'story', 'plot', and 'pattern and rhythm' constitute the beginning, middle and end of his essay, and are important in an ascending order. They are interdependent, and it is quite clear that Forster's preference is for 'pattern and rhythm', words which he happily draws not from the past of literary theories but from painting and music. 'Pattern' creates a pictorial image and hence a new geometry, and he immediately begins talking about novels shaped like an hour-glass (Anatole France's *Thais*, James's *The Ambassadors*) or like a chain (Percy Lubbock's *Roman Pictures*). 'Rhythm' with its musical evocation is not geometric but has some of the same satisfying qualities: it 'may be defined as repetition plus variations' (p. 154) and is best defined by Proust's novel then in process of publication: 'The book is chaotic, ill constructed, it has and will have no external shape; and yet it hangs together because it is stitched internally, because it contains rhythms' (p. 151).

Much more recently, Alvin B. Kernan has added to our stock-pile of plot shapes by his classifications in *The Plot of Satire*. Although such critics as Ronald Paulson (*The Fictions of Satire*) would claim that 'However much mimesis or representation is involved, the generic end [of satire] is rhetorical' (p. 3). Kernan's image of satire is pictorial and plot-centred. He builds his thesis of the importance of plotted satiric modes on Swift's statement in *A Tale of a Tub*, Section VIII:

And, whereas the mind of Man, when he gives the Spur and Bridle to his Thoughts, doth never stop, but naturally sallies out into both extreams of High and Low, of Good and Evil; His first Flight of Fancy, commonly transports Him to Ideas of what is most Perfect, finished, and exalted: till having soared out of his own Reach and Sight, not well perceiving how near the Frontiers of Height and Depth, border upon each other; With the same Course and Wing, he falls down plum into the lowest Bottom of Things; like one who travels the *East* into the *West*; or like a strait Line drawn by its own Length into a Circle.

From these images of rising and falling, and transformation of line to circle, supplemented by what he calls the 'Everything-Nothing' pattern of, for example, *The Dunciad*, he builds a view of plot as a shape made and held by the active force of all literature. Perhaps this shape is, after all, a more symbolic and more literary reading of what Aristotle meant when he said the writer must keep the action before his eyes.

TIME

Plot is the arrangement of action; action progresses through the indispensable medium of time from which it derives all of its modifying vocabularies. Beginning, middle, and end constitute a march through temporal history, and causality exists in flux. Nothing could be simpler, and no single aspect of literature has become more subject to re-thinking, philosophical doubt, anthropological disproving, and intellectual experimentation. The capacity for resting an aesthetic image of time in the Spenserian Garden of Adonis where 'eterne in mutabilitie' can be found was destroyed by the internal realizations of the Cartesian moment. The fictions of both prose and poetry have been increasingly tormented by the denials of time as measurable, predictable, and exterior. To deny time is to destroy conventional form, which must then be re-created in accordance with whatever method the mind was chosen for its confrontation with temporality.

In distinguishing time from temporality, we are confronting the one of primary features of the vast discussion. Time as history, the progression of minutes, hours, days, measurable by clock and calendar, has little to do with the primordial processes of temporality, a word which in its present usage is borrowed from Martin Heidegger's *Being and Time* and altered to fit the literary occasion. In Heidegger's thinking, the untranslatable *Dasein* (da-sein, to be there – the central existing of the mind) in seeking its totality (first through its being-towards-death) discovers temporality as real and as an agent. We know without Heidegger's help that the idea of being itself is temporal as are all verb forms, but temporality is nevertheless an inner 'existentiall' discovery and separated from time as history, which – to simplify greatly and perhaps to confuse – is created through the temporalizing of temporality.

In transferring the term temporality into literature, we are led to a discovery quite separated from philosophical discourse: temporality becomes a vehicle of comprehension and therefore approximates the quality of metaphor. As soon as temporality – as a means of presenting a private vision of where and how action exists – became current, it was seized as an instrument of criticism and helped the critic to understand the noncausal designs which erupted as reactions against what had been known or thought about form. As a critical movement, its ramifications have been widespread, but literature itself is still in the vanguard as it seeks to find new times and new forms.

E. M. Forster talked about the movement with practicality and innocence, because he had not thought philosophically about Proust and because he was not attempting to prophesy the contours of literary criticism in the twentieth century:

> . . . in a novel there is always a clock. The author may dislike his clock. Emily Brontë in *Wuthering Heights* tried to hide hers. Sterne, in *Tristram Shandy*, turned his upside down. Marcel Proust, still more ingenious, kept altering the hands, so that his hero was at the same period entertaining a mistress to supper and playing ball with his

nurse in the park. All these devices are legitimate, but none of them contravene our thesis: the basis of a novel is a story, and a story is a narrative of events arranged in time sequence.

(p. 31)

This is an old-fashioned refusal to see two times, or to distinguish between what can be termed time and temporality, but Forster instinctively knew that something had happened to the root idea of plot and/or story. He is dissatisfied with the old form of an end, and tries to devise a new idea which he thought peculiar to the novel form:

> After all, why has a novel to be planned? Cannot it grow? Why need it close, as a play closes? Cannot it open out? Instead of standing above his work and controlling it, cannot the novelist throw himself into it and be carried along to some goal that he does not foresee? The plot is exciting and may be beautiful, yet is it not a fetich, borrowed from the drama, from the spatial limitations of the stage? Cannot fiction devise a framework that is not so logical yet more suitable to its genius?

(pp. 92–93)

In embryonic state, this is the theory which leads to the critical idea of open forms, to the denial of endings, to the opening out of action as opposed to the formal closing that older ideas of an ending legislated. It must be pointed out that criticism got there much later than literature – *Tristram Shandy* is, as usual, the universal example – but even as Forster wrote, it had become something close to commonplace in practice.

Once the problems of time and its interpretations are posited, their ramifications become almost infinite. In Chapter 1 of *Mimesis*, Erich Auerbach talks about the incident of Odysseus' Scar in the *Odyssey* and compares its temporal presentation with the Genesis account of Abraham's willingness to sacrifice Isaac. Both are epic accounts, but are clearly separated in style because of the arrangement of time and its background. Odysseus, although unrecognized on his return to Ithaca, is having his feet washed by his ancient nurse, who suddenly sees the scar and recognizes its bearer. At this moment, there is a flashback telling the history of the scar, of Odysseus' grandfather Autolycus whom the young hero was visiting when the wound was incurred during a boar-hunt, and of the anxiety of his parents, before returning to the moment in Penelope's chamber. Auerbach claims that this is a specific example of the Homeric style, and not a method of increasing suspense; 'the Homeric style knows only a foreground, only a uniformly illuminated, uniformly objective present . . . the story of the wound becomes an independent and exclusive present' (p. 5). This form of foreground writing, 'in a local and temporal present which is absolute' (p. 4), is contrasted with the sparse, background-dependent style of the Abraham story. Details of time and place are not precisely revealed, and the narrative point lies in its barrenness:

> The world of the Scripture stories is not satisfied with claiming to be a historically true reality – it insists that it is the only real world, is destined for autocracy. . . . The Scripture stories do not, like Homer's court our favor, they do not flatter us that they may please us and enchant us – they seek to subject us, and if we refuse to be subjected we are rebels . . . the stories are not, like Homer's simply narrated 'reality'. Doctrine and promise are incarnate in them; for that very reason, they are fraught with 'background' and mysterious, containing a second, concealed meaning.
>
> (p. 12)

John Barth, in his 'Menelaiad' (in *Lost in the Funhouse*, 1969) takes us past the security of these contrasted forms to the final modern absurdity, where narrated reality loses its eternal present and its authority in the mazes of time. Like the authors of both the *Odyssey* and Genesis, his mimetic theme is epic, and he is ultimately concerned with narrative possibilities. All of the semi-connected narratives 'for print, tape, live voice' in *Lost in the*

Funhouse may be described as practical experiments in plot as it exists after the invasion of time theories. Much of the self-defeating wit of the 'Menelaid' is reflected in what Barth labels the 'Frame-Tale' of the book, pp. 1–2. It is meant to be cut out with scissors and joined at the ends to form a little circle of paper, on one side of which is printed 'ONCE UPON A TIME THERE', and on the other, 'WAS A STORY THAT BEGAN'. As it is twirled, the reader is in an eternal cycle of plot within plot which would read like this: 'Once upon a time there was a story that began once upon a time there was a story that began . . .'' *ad infinitum*, or until one understands that what is being expressed is the mad whirligig of time as the narrator realizes he is not twice removed from the reality he ought to imitate as Plato had suggested, but infinitely separated and unable to detach himself from the temporal, circular externals and get on with real narration. In other words, there can be no actual plot, only the twirling formula of conventional beginning.

In the 'Menelaid', there is an attempt at Homeric foreground, but the trap of multiplied layers of time, of the progressive separations which time imposes on narrative, quickly takes over. Menelaus begins, talking to himself, but realizes suddenly that he has an audience and starts consciously telling the tale of his return after the fall of Troy (the point seems to be that it is the narrator's self-consciousness, his awareness of himself as narrating subject, which begins the insane problem) – a circumstance which justifies one set of quotation marks. Then he is telling us that he is telling the tale to Telemachus and Peisistratus, then he tells us he is telling them he is telling Helen, then he tells us he is telling Telemachus and Peisistratus he is telling Helen he is telling Proteus, then Eidothea, until he is firmly stuck at one moment. Progress and development only tie the narrative more tightly and hopelessly and the eye of the reader scans, with desperate confusion, a devastating, anti-communicative series of quotation marks:

""""""*Why?*' I repeated," I repeated,' I repeated," I repeated,' I
repeated," I repeat. """"""" And the woman, with a bride-shy smile
and hushèd voice, replied: 'Why what?'

(p. 152)

The thing is erudite, madly funny, and a firm lesson about time
and plot.

The place of time in the narrative and its potential control over
the structure of fictions has a lengthy background and is typified
by the Romantic melancholy of Keats and his poem's confrontation
with the 'sole self' after the flight of the nightingale, or the spent
Chateaubriandesque hero sadly kicking his way through the
autumnal leaves. Its overwhelming incursion came, however, with
the publication of Marcel Proust's *A la Recherche du Temps Perdu*
where Time is both theme and vehicle and where no chronology
operates except that controlled by the moving mind and will of
the narrator, Marcel. Stream of consciousness is not an adequate
way of describing the processes involved in this virtually epoch-
making work, although all works which we label with that term
are in some way interpreting the interior clock of the mind as
opposed to the flux of history.

Comprehension of temporality begins for Proust in the memory,
for he, like Nabokov, gives artistic credence only to time past or
painfully present and does not involve himself in optimistic posi-
tivism. In fact, the future contains only anguish-creating transitions
or the sluggishness of habitual action. The writing of the book (or
books, you may choose singularity or plurality) is not an aesthetic
but a philosophical exercise. As such, its pursuit of meaning and
very shape constitute an ontological study whose outcome is a
definition of the possibilities of the mind relative to its experiences.
As the narrator reviews his past, the major feature is his constant
wretchedness and maladjustment whenever the physical surround-
ing of his life change or whenever, because of the passage of time,
his bliss in being with his mother or being kissed by her is removed

as she sits for some hours with other adults rather than atemporally bestowing her eternal radiance on him. The latter problem reflects his horror at the very fact of flux, but the earlier has to do with a central recognition of human behaviour also involved in the idea of time. In a most trenchant commentary on Proust, Samuel Beckett locates this overpowering malaise in the painful periods of transition between the dull insensitivity of habit (what George Eliot in the very different context of *Middlemarch* called the wadding of stupidity which keeps us from hearing the squirrel's heart beat or the grass grow) and the 'suffering of being' (p. 19). As consciousness absorbs the forms of its material setting, it becomes increasingly desensitized and hence comfortable. Anguish occurs when awareness of reality is in operation; comfort is a quality of insensitivity and habit.

Proust's personal experiment also teaches the reader the relative smallness of the achievements of the voluntary memory – that is, the will to remember the past and to make connections which might help illuminate one's being. The voluntary memory can recreate but does so usually in terms of perversion or transformation – again, a blunting of reality rather than the thing itself. It is the involuntary memory alone which cannot be called into action by the will, that floods the mind with sharp reality and causes essential knowledge – what Beckett calls 'astral synthesis' (p. 61). This knowledge transcends time and its dolours and, because death is an aspect of time, defeats even that. The tragedy lies in the momentary nature of this knowledge, in the mind's instant and necessary return to flux and to its own unsuccessful efforts.

The length and structure of these voluntary attempts form or do the active plotting of the novel. In other words, the plot is shaped not by literary theories but by an unremitting philosophical quest. Proust's inquiry into time and being concurred with existential phenomenology, and has maintained currency as both a

philosophical and technical factor in literature. It also opened out
the question of the identity of the created fiction. Forster said
that the story is everything, but here is proof that the story is a
lagging second to the mental search, that temporality can take
over the dynamics and become what Aristotle called the soul of
the work of literature.

Increasingly, the idea of fiction has become, not mythologized
into categories as Northrop Frye and his followers have explained
it, but enlarged to include thought patterns through which we
attempt to find truth. This is a withdrawal both from the art-for-
art's-sake school and from the pedantries of mimetic realism to the
assertion of art for the mind's sake, art as a quest for and repository
of whatever ultimate reality the mind can achieve. In one of his
adages, Wallace Stevens, whose notes towards a supreme fiction
are very good ones, put it this way: 'The final belief is to believe
in a fiction, which you know to be a fiction, there being nothing
else. The exquisite truth is to know that it is a fiction and that
you believe in it willingly.'

When temporality assumes such power as a shaping and controlling element, we are reminded to reconsider the literature of
the past in the light of what our present has discovered. Both the
flux of time and temporality have been with us since the garland
of roses first faded in Adam's hand, and one way of approaching
both literature and the life of the mind which literature expresses
is through an historical examination of man's changing or evolving
comprehension of time. In this connection, two major critical
works can be stressed as dominant histories of the idea – Georges
Poulet, *Études sur le Temps Humain* and Frank Kermode, *The
Sense of an Ending*.

Poulet's work reflects thought in progress: he sees the comprehension of time changing from the medieval confidence in God's
creation and unceasing recreation of the world to the seventeenth
century's recognition of the isolation of the individual. He develops

a sense of change through Bergsonian theories of perpetual *durée* to the twentieth century concept of the instant, which he illustrates most successfully in Gidean terms as the 'moment sensible', and identifies with Kierkegaard's 'moment esthétique' (Vol. III, p. 9). The task or dream of Gide's art as exemplary is to escape history through a succession of such moments of intensity, the creation of a world of his own. Poulet's method is not as limited as these brief sentences would indicate, for he works creatively through the works, structures, and ideas of many writers and by indirection encourages in his readers the study of more and more thinkers in the accumulation of developing ideas of time.

Kermode's is the more polished and far-ranging study, as his data-collecting includes theology, sociology, philosophy, and the other agents of fiction-producing thought. In one sense he is expanding Aristotle's ideas about plot, and is concerned with what has happened to endings in particular, but middles as well. As for beginnings – well, he mentions Genesis, but there can be no doubt that literature as he views it is preoccupied with the other aspects of that famous and sensible triad. The force of Kermode's analysis is not primarily in literature alone, but in the cultural complex from which literature took, at various times, its method and focus. He begins with Christian ideas of apocalypse and the variations of thought and experience which modified it, and ends with 'solitary confinement', a dazzling study of what the mind does when it is literally isolated and utterly without exterior fiction-producing props. Between this beginning and conclusion is an examination of medieval *aevum*, of modern crisis, of life (and, through the logic of his extensions, literature as well) in time and in what he calls 'the middest'.

This broadened base of literary criticism under the aegis of time comes not only from philosophy, but from the enlarging ideas which anthropological studies have brought to bear on our thinking. In one such study, *The Myth of the Eternal Return*, Mircea Eliade presents us with a vital phrase, *illud tempus*, which does much to explain primordial human rituals and their translation into something more sophisticated in literature. His anthropological observations of archaic man reveal methods by which history is abolished and the comforts of atemporality attained. Because of the reiterated revival of archetypes, linear history holds no threats. Thus archaic man, by positing a belief in some ancient golden season of the gods, performs the crucial actions in life as a ritual which imitates the same action first performed and projected into archetype by the gods *in illo tempore*, before the world dwindled into the place of mere men. This action as imitated by man is fused in one eternal moment: every time the community reperforms the action, it destroys time and recreates that first archetypal moment literally, thus partaking of an eternal present. Another form of the same idea occurs when rites for the new year are cyclically celebrated, with the result that man instead of progressing through the line of history renews it – goes back and starts all over again from the beginning. When eschatological thinking occurs, *illud tempus* – the archetypal time of the gods – not only exists in the golden past but can be restored in the future, so that what man knows as profane time is a hiatus between the two real times of the archetype.

As Eliade points out, there has been a growing desire in twentieth century literature to recapture the cycle and religious centre of *illud tempus* (he mentions specifically T. S. Eliot and Joyce, but this list could be greatly expanded) as the terrors of freedom and evolutionary theories of time are less and less supportable for the psyche. Henri Focillon (in *The Life of Forms in Art*) refers to the same instinct when he talks about man's quite unjustified tendency to think in terms of the 'color and physiognomy' of a century and to indulge in '"centurial" mysticism' (p. 54).

As we have thought more and more extensively about the mind's various discoveries of temporality, we have been forced to wean ourselves from the simpler forms of history. Increasingly more of the data of time has been rejected from art theory in an attempt to get at its real subject. Let us give Focillon the last word on the irrelevance of date and chronology to either history or the definition of art in history:

> The historian who reads events in sequence also reads them in breadth, synchronously, as the musician reads a full orchestral score. History is not unilinear; it is not pure sequence. We may best regard it as the superimposition of very widely spaced moments ... At the same date, politics, economics, and art do not occupy identical positions on their respective graphs, and the line joining them at any one given moment is more often than not a very irregular one. In theory, we readily admit this; in practice, we give way to our need for some pre-established harmony, that is, for regarding the date as a focus, a point within which everything is concentrated. And yet, even though the date may indeed be such a point, it is not so by definition. History is, in general, a conflict among what is precocious, actual, or merely delayed.

(p. 55)

4
Practical Plotting

'Aristotle is a skeleton.' – *Adagia*, Wallace Stevens

Our subject to this point has been theory – theory in theory and theory in practice – and the agreement or opposition one may find in contemplating that theory. Our acquaintance with literature is always much more immediate, and doubtless our best thinking about the nature and function of a term like plot will arise from an intimate relationship with texts in which plot is an integral part, not a separate theory of critic or philosopher. Every work with the movement of *mythos* creates the necessity of a special, detailed consideration – a task which cannot be even approximated within the next few pages. Let us, rather, assemble some eclectic notes which contribute to what we can know about the way plotting is actually carried out and what it looks like when it is finished or even partly finished. It is finally the actual works of literature which fill out or crumble the skeleton of theory, and it would be idle to talk about plot without making some gestures in this direction.

It is pointless to be interested in hack work like Dumas' hiring of friends to prepare plot outlines in vast quantity to be filled out later so that his stuff could keep rolling off the press. Good literature must be considered, and time is better spent in such exercises as that neoclassical pursuit suggested by Dryden – tracking Ben Jonson through the snow to his recognizable ancient sources. It is useful to examine the plot stockpile at any given period (as a means of gauging the nature of artistic discovery and also to work against the kind of casual remarks – like the Leavisite statement of parallelism between Dickens and George Eliot –

which are tossed off because of imperfect examination of what plots and themes are current), to study individual scenes and their parallels at other moments in the work, to check the dynamics of juxtapositions and metaphors, and to examine the interconnections of idea and form, which James called the needle and thread of fiction. Every piece of literature asks that we perform this service, and we must acquiesce.

ECLECTIC EXAMPLES

Plotting evolves a law of its own in terms of audience interest: the more complex the structure of the fiction, the greater our interest in finding out how it got that way. Theories about plot and new vocabularies are an objectification of the attempt to satisfy this hunger to know, to get to the root of the art, to lay bare the substance of composition. The artist who can be tracked in the snow because of his use of conventional forms or whose plot is simple and logical gives satisfaction fairly directly, but there remains the writer who does not yield so easily and whom we pursue with questions which must constantly be revised. If the right questions can be found, some answers at least will follow. Seldom is the reader satisfied to accept the totality of the finished work, and therefore he involves himself in the tantalizing quest after artistic process.

There is a certain kind of practical historico-literary book which helps considerably in the preliminary stages of inquiry into the 'how' of plotting. Such books as W. P. Ker's *Epic and Romance*, Samuel Lee Wolff's *The Greek Romances in Elizabethan Prose Fiction*, T. W. Baldwin's *Shakespeare's Five-Act Structure*, the studies of source and analogue in Shakespeare's plays by Geoffrey Bullough and Kenneth Muir, to list only a few, assist in defining the compositions we may be involved in examining. Unfortunately, they are dependent on a literature which flourishes in a period of humanist continuity where it can be taken for granted that genres exist and borrowing of plot and technique is common-place. Nabokov's complex *Ada* or Joyce's *Ulysses*, for example, cannot be unravelled in the same traditional manner: an over-arching continuum like a five-act structure is of little value, and even the history of saga or epic is far removed from the questions raised by such new and multiform works. Even when this type of book helps, its contribution is at best partial and often prior to the search the reader feels impelled to undertake.

The desire to unravel and make sense of the writer's composi-tional progress through his work is not new, but must constantly be reiterated and revised according to the tastes and knowledge of different generations. A highly entertaining seventeenth-century example is Thomas Rymer's struggles with Shakespeare's *Othello* in his *A Short View of Tragedy*. Like Tolstoi, Rymer is not a fan and has no intention of descending into even the first circle of bardolatry. His basic neo-classicism has convinced him that *Othello* is bad, and his method of proving it involves a step-by-step examination of the plot so that from compositional moment to moment he can show its heinous and continual smashing of veri-similitude and decorum. In other words, his attention is focused not on a general, over-all view, but on the plotting and progression of the work as it accumulates outrages. His intention is to have the reader see how utterly mad Shakespeare was from scene to scene, from character to character, from idea to idea.

Since the nineteenth-century revivals of Shakespeare, there is little tendency to want to repeat or agree with Rymer's point of view, but Shakespeare's plays remain among the most elusive and tantalizing structures we have. It is his silence on the subject of his work – or on any other subject – which raises anxiety to such a pitch, and to assuage it many readers have argued that the words he puts into the mouth of his characters are in fact his own expressions. When that fallacy is avoided, others are substituted, such as assigning monumental power to the sources and saying that Shakespeare nodded in translating them to his own drama, or arguing from what is ultimately intuition and intentional fallacy. The only slender indications we in fact have of his compositional processes occur in differences between quartos (as in the challenging evidence of the two *Hamlets*) or quarto and folio. Even here there is much doubt, as twentieth-century textual scholarship indicates, but the rest is unavoidable, impelling questions and educated guesses.

At every point of composition, Shakespeare's plays raise extensive questions. Nor is there any assurance that there is a simple intention behind those moments when he seems to be most conventional. For example, both *Merchant of Venice* and *Measure for Measure* end in accordance with common formulae for the conclusion of comedy. Shylock is ousted from the stage wretchedly in *Merchant of Venice* on the eve of his enforced conversion, and all of Act V reverts to moon-washed Belmont, to Jessica and Lorenzo, the ring game and its resolution, and the harmony of paired couples. The conventions are met, the concord of marriage completes the happy device of comic endings, but both theatregoer and reader are aware that there is an active plot beneath the conventional aura of wholeness which has not been satisfied and which infuses any interpretation which might be given to the play. Shylock has been translated from comic villain to a powerful new dimension, and in the middle of the triumphant love in marriage celebrations at the end, Antonio is as much the outsider, the 'tainted wether of the flock', as he had been in Act IV when Portia effected the *peripeteia* of Shylock's plan. This is a case of plot countering plot, or of unresolved intrusions co-existing with the smooth patina of the consoling and accepted form.

Measure for Measure offers the same complexity of convention overlaid with its denial, a repetition which ought to convince that the technique of *Merchant of Venice* was not a fluke and not entirely an example of Shakespeare's inability to handle the strength and connotations of the action which he had set in motion. Here, too, the conventions are met, and the play ends with a procession of marriages – Angelo and Mariana, Claudio and Juliet, Lucio and his bawd, and probably Isabella and the Duke, although she is not assigned a verbal reply to his proposing couplets. Under the concord lies its contrary, for aside from the union of Claudio and Juliet, there is radical *mésalliance* in each of the marriages: Angelo is ready for any punishment, preferably death, and is fulfilling a heavy duty in his marriage to Mariana, poor Lucio is appalled at marrying anything so base as a bawd, and Isabella who had once wished that the sisters of St. Clare had more stringent prohibitions placed on their order is belying the consistency of her character and falsifying the moral position she had held throughout the play. One may conjecture that in both of these plays Shakespeare is not only creating works that are morally problematic but employing the instrument of the drama to experiment with doubleness and complexities of plot, and to layer technique so that the antinomies of established convention and irreducible innovation co-exist.

Equally interesting in terms of practical examinations of Shakespeare's plotting is the study of his opening exposition. Because of the sanctity in which the process of the plays is generally held, there has been a tendency to make the techniques of beginnings much too dull and matter-of-fact. No one who has seen several productions of *Twelfth Night* can avoid being struck by the strangeness of the Duke Orsino's long opening semi-soliloquy as music is played to him. Not only does the staging of the scene require vast ingenuity, but very few actors of whatever skill are able to carry off the puzzling *préciosité* of the luxurious Duke. Textual analyses and thematic connections offer help, but the questions which are raised go beyond the limits of these ideological exercises. In the fastest-paced of his comedies, why did Shakepeare begin with this almost unplayable languor? What, precisely, constitutes the mechanics of his plot and why has he used this method of beginning it?

Or, to use still another example, what is the rationale behind the plotting of the first three scenes of *Richard II*? In production, Scene ii often precedes Scene i, thus explaining the puzzling factors in Scene i as it stands. Scene ii presents a convenient scene of explanatory exposition between the Duchess of Gloucester and John of Gaunt, announcing Richard's guilt, partly through the agency of Mowbray, in the death of his uncle Gloucester. Had Shakespeare intended the play to open with this scene, the fraudulence of Richard's character in both the challenge scene and the tournament sequence would be palpable and immediate to the audience, even granting that they did not know the commonplace historical gossip. There is, moreover, the question of why two scenes, Scene i of challenge and Scene iii of tournament, had to be carried out when one alone could have borne the burden of action for both. The beginning of an answer can be found in the fact that Shakespeare wanted to expose the ritual, duplicity, and verbal insight of Richard before he allowed a scene which would point the finger of guilt at him. Scene i is impressive and puzzling; every speech of each major character is covered with layers of deceit and indirection. As a result, the audience quickly recognizes that it is dealing with language and its possibilities rather than action which is both veiled and indirect. Scene ii presents an edge of everyday truth, so that when the focal action continues in Scene iii the audience has learned the very subtle science of modification. It is a brilliant technique and one which defines the normative value of the entire play, where indirection rather than direction seeks out whatever truth lies in human behaviour.

Although Shakespeare delivered no prose exposition of how and why he plotted his work, some of his near contemporaries made movements in that direction, and it is with a sigh of gratitude that we look at the explanatory documents of Sidney and Spenser.

In his famous letter to Sir Walter Ralegh, dated 23 January, 1589, Spenser set out a brief explanation of his *Faerie Queene* which began publication in 1590, 'to direct your understanding to the wel-head of the history, that from thence gathering the whole intention of the conceit, ye may, as in a handfull, gripe al the discourse, which otherwise may happily seeme tedious and confused.' It is indeed a neat handful, based in intention on the twelve moral virtues of Aristotle, each of which would receive a book of the allegory. Spenser knew that comprehension could not be clear from the first three books he published which were fascinatingly work in progress:

> The beginning therefore of my history, if it were to be told by an historiographer, should be the twelfth booke, which is the last; where I devise that the Faery Queene kept her annuall feaste xii. dayes, uppon which xii. several dayes, the occasions of the xii. severall adventures hapned, which being undertaken by xii. severall knights, are in these xii. book severally handled and discoursed.

Most readers are quite ready to credit his account of the churlish young knight lounging rustically about the court of Gloriana until Una appears, at which point he dons the Christian armour of Ephesians and becomes the gentle knight of Book I, but no amount of credibility or compositional and/or intentional gymnastics can explain Spenser's distortion of Book II and its utter opposition to the composed text. The account of Book III is equally upended. The explanatory letter will not persuade even the casual reader of Book III that the hero is Scudamour and not Britomart, nor is Spenser's sequence correct in Book II – the Palmer does not bring Ruddymane to the court and then collect Guyon, but rather he and Guyon come upon Mordant and Amavia, the latter tells the tale of Acrasia as her swan-song, and the blood-stained child is delivered to them.

Spenser's explanations have caused as much conflict and questioning as Shakespeare's silence. It has been conjectured by

Josephine Waters Bennett (*The Evolution of 'The Faerie Queene*, Chicago, 1942) that Spenser's plot seems inaccurate so often because he did not compose it consecutively, but wrote haphazardly and then joined the sections together with what logic he could muster. Contrary arguments have been put forward to assure the Spenserian enthusiast that everything would reach its ultimate order on the completion of the twelve books. As we have only six, all of our arguments must assume truncation and process, and we must acknowledge the inexplicable gap between prose intention and poetic accomplishment.

Sir Philip Sidney is at first still more comforting, as he gives us a *Defence of Poesie* and two versions of an *Arcadia* which share the essentials of plot outline. The *Defence* has absorbed Aristotle, Plato, Horace, and the Italian interpreters; its impulse is moral and, like Spenser, Sidney would have literature perform the function of shaping through example the character of the ideal man. His most important concepts have to do with the concept of a 'fore conceit' and the formulation of what he calls a golden world and opposes to the brazen world of other intellectual disciplines and of experience. The 'fore conceit' is a Platonic idea and exists above the actual work of art: it appears to be what the poet envisions before the actual scribbling begins. Sidney's own creative habits indicate the difficulties he encountered in trying to work his plot into the detail and final form he wanted. Having completed one *Arcadia* as a five-act structure in traditional form, he began recasting, enlarging and superimposing new plot contours and copious subplots on the basic work. Here again the reader confronts the primary question of how and to what end this revision was undertaken. Is it a pursuit of the almost unattainable 'fore conceit'? What in the basic plot evoked the insistent need to start again? Sidney's *Defence* tells us something, the fact of revision reveals even more, but the thirst of curiosity remains. The Renaissance kept its secrets well.

By the nineteenth century, the grand century of the novel, certain exterior conditions come to the assistance of our query into the ways and means of planning and writing fiction. Publishing conditions were such that most novels were issued first in periodicals, chapter by chapter, or in separate monthly parts containing three or four chapters each, with the result that the concept of chapter became an impressive form in itself. Needless to say, such publication did not always have good effects. It produced the very long novel which stretched the audience's imagination over month after month and kept up sales of the journal or monthly parts in question. To keep instalments interesting, novelists were too often forced into melodramatic modes, coincidences and intrigues which read like crossword puzzles, and the creation of crises so numerous that bathos is too often approximated and more often reached. As a profitable bourgeois system, it can be incorrectly blamed for the bad novelists of the Victorian period, but it must also share the triumph of the big novel as an astonishing popular and artistic achievement. Dickens' brilliantly original and idiosyncratic style is doubtless the product partly of the conditions under which he wrote, and Trollope's expansive and ironic handling of plot has the same origins. It is a circumstance designed for the pleasures of complexity and multiple plots, and offers ample opportunity for the exciting use of the elements of recognition and reversal urged by Aristotle.

The expansiveness of the nineteenth-century style encouraged spreading of idea and above all the plenitude of realistic theory which produced such writers as Zola, and Balzac's large rendering of human life in *La Comédie Humaine*. The very fact that realism was a new movement meant that it had to be defended against the traditionalists, and the novelists of realism began to publish more about the direct process of writing than had generally been available before. Even more advantageous from our standpoint, the writer of the big novel usually began with a notebook, journal, elaborated plan, many of which were preserved and are, increasingly, considered important matter for publication by modern scholars.

The nineteenth century did not have the eager, non-selective desire to see every scrap of an artist's handwriting committed to print which characterizes our century. Dickens would not have been enticed into publishing his journal of *Hard Times* in the way Gide did his of *Les Faux-Monnayeurs* as a dependent but additional art form. Nevertheless, the preservation of these notebooks of various writers and the illumination that, for example, is given to Dostoevsky's *Crime and Punishment* from their current scholarly publication are invaluable to our continuing interest in plotting techniques. In addition, the habit of publishing letters has gone on apace, and we can glean compositional material and attitudes from these.

The exercise of reconstructing how the nineteenth-century novelist worked is fascinating. Although it is a task which most of us jealously regard as a personal part of our creative reading, it is still useful to examine how one scholar, with journals, manuscripts, letters, printed editions and extensive patience uncovers the step-by-step process of planning and writing a major novel. In *'Middlemarch' from Notebook to Novel*, Jerome Beaty judiciously traces the elements of George Eliot's work on *Middlemarch* from its inception early in 1869 to its publication in 1872.

Originally George Eliot planned a novel to be called *Middlemarch* whose subject would be that town and the story of the young doctor Lydgate. By March 19, 1871, she had fused two stories both in process – the original *Middlemarch* and the story of 'Miss Brooke' which included the Casaubon and Ladislaw threads – into what she described as 236 pages of print. Always aware of the difficulties of his task, Beaty follows her through the revisions which fusion entailed, cautiously presenting the evidence of spacing of handwriting, corrections, and the water-marks of the paper she used at different times, in the best style of the literary sleuth:

> Between the day of decision, Dec. 31, 1870, or soon thereafter, and March 19, 1871, when George Eliot had completed 236 pages of the now joined *Middlemarch*, lay innumerable possibilities and consequently innumerable small decisions, a vast amount of rethinking and replanning, some rewriting, and some new writing in order to make the two separate stories fuse smoothly. There lies for us, consequently, a vast amount of surmising, assuming, deducing, and reconstructing.
>
> (p. 11)

His analysis includes a detailed surmise of what probably happened, followed by an examination of the influence on her composition of Lewes' idea to make the book into a four-volume work as its length demanded rather than keeping it limited to the habitual three volumes, and to issue these four volumes in eight parts over a substantial period of time. The chapter on her notebook illustrates the creative disparity between her plan and the act of transferring it to the completed prose of the novel. At every step, Beaty has used great discretion in stripping the components of the novel which existed before and during the writing, and the result is a book which satisfies the modern reader's craving to know.

The twentieth century has taken us further still into the process of art, because the artist himself is obsessed with it. The product orientation which causes the literary person to look at the work itself is constantly being supplemented by what the artist is more than willing to reveal about himself while writing. These revelations, to name only a few, range from the anguish of D. H. Lawrence's attempts to remake *The Rainbow*, to Gide's spiritual voyage in *Journal des Faux-Monnayeurs*. Thomas Mann has also given his account of the making of *Doctor Faustus* in a document of the highest philosophical statement and inquiry, *Die Entstehung des Doktor Faustus*.

As an example of the desire to reveal the artistic process, Gide's *Journal* is convenient. In *Les Faux-Monnayeurs* itself, his artist character, Edouard, passionately describes the idea of the journal which he is later to claim is even more interesting than the novel, and wishes that every great novel had one accompanying it:

> ... it's a kind of diary that I keep as one might do of a child. ... That is to say, that instead of contenting myself with resolving each difficulty as it presents itself (and every work of art is only the sum or the product of the solutions of a quantity of small difficulties), I set forth each of these difficulties and study it. My notebook contains, as it were, a running criticism of my novel – or rather of the novel in general. Just think how interesting such a notebook kept by Dickens or Balzac would be; if we had the diary of the *Education Sentimentale* or of *The Brothers Karamazof*! – the story of the work – of its gestation! How thrilling it would be ... more interesting than the work itself.
>
> (p. 170, Penguin ed. *The Counterfeiters*, translated by Dorothy Bussy, Harmondsworth, 1966)

The *Journal*, covering Gide's anxious thinking about the novel, is dedicated thus: 'J'offre ces cahiers d'exercices et d'études à mon ami Jacques de Lacretelle et à ceux que les questions de métier intéressent.' The study of his craft covers the lengthy period from 17 June 1919 to May 1925. He talks about practical problems such as the dating of the novel – a story about counterfeit coins must take place before World War I, after which gold coins were abolished – or his desire (unrealized) that the story which becomes young Georges' theft under Edouard's eyes be told by the child and not the novelist. When *ennui* and despair set in, he records it, and announces the advice or arguments of Martin de Gard or Claudel. At one point late in composition, the proofs of his translation of Fielding arrive, and he is overcome by his own inadequacy. It is not until page 51 (premier cahier) that he begins writing, but for this novel very much in process and ultimately unfinishable, everything is desperately difficult. This difficulty must find expression through Edouard who is made (p. 67) to talk in contradictions and always differently about the way the novel is constructed.

An important revelation is given when Gide admits that he can write with greater freedom when he assumes the personality of someone who is considerably different from himself – like the character of Lafcadio. Here in *Les Faux Monnayeurs* he allows himself Edouard, Bernard, Olivier and the fraudulent Comte de Passavant, and he finds that gradually his novel takes on a force of its own, like an organic plant which cannot be forced but which works forward with nature (pp. 89–90). Throughout the *Journal*, there is a stream stronger than nature – that of diabolism. Gide sees this as affecting most of his characters but he purifies it in the actuality of the novel into a new, subtle tone, except where it is allowed direct range in the character of old La Pérouse. Most importantly of all, he reveals the reality on which the plot is based and which it transforms, even giving appendices from *Le Figaro* and the *Journal de Rouen* about the original counterfeit coins and the suicide of schoolboys. His character Bernard interprets this in the novel:

'But why start from an idea?' interrupted Bernard impatiently. 'If you were to start from a fact and make a good exposition of it, the idea would come of its own accord to inhabit it. If I were writing *The Counterfeiters* I should begin by showing the counterfeit coin – the little ten-franc piece you were speaking of just now.'

But this is not the method – the straightforwardness of Bernard is not the active technique in the novel Gide envisages, and which his journal enriches so immeasurably. As in the case of the novel, the *Journal* does not produce an image of completion, and the eternal present of Gide's complex revelations carry us to that middle distance where Gide would locate reality. All of its ramifications, particular and general, he would generously convey to his ideal, working reader, and we devour it greedily.

5
Conclusion

The hardest thing to draw. Serious contemplation of a term like plot of necessity calls elaborate attention to critics and theorists whose progressive ideational developments must be absorbed by the word, and by any one wishing to use and understand the complex ramifications it spawns. More significantly, it is a word which establishes a liaison between reader and literary text, demanding that each reader comprehend the active principle which the fiction being considered creates. In other words, it is a term which, when justly used, asks that every reader participate in the movement of the form and through this participation become himself a critic. Its stress and life are nevertheless in the work of literature – in its interior dynamics.

Crucial to any conclusions which might be drawn is the very real fact that the traditional bad reputation of plot in its simplest definition has led to the inability of the word to stand alone without the expanding force of vocabulary increase. The purpose of this monograph has been to lead the reader from the standard definition of plot as a hackneyed mechanical term to its enormous possibilities in the primary Aristotelian description as the action which is the soul of fiction. Modern expansions of the literary vocabulary should be attached to it and should be themselves expanded, and increasing absorption of chiliastic, anthropological, or mediumistic advances will change it more. Plot should be seen as a term capable of indefinite growth and alteration. Like modern literary works, it too is very much in process: it both defines and is action.

Bibliography

ADAMS, ROBERT M., *Strains of Discord: Studies in Literary Openness*, Ithaca, New York, 1958.
Valuable for its description of open and closed fictional forms.

ARISTOTLE, *Poetics*, Loeb edition, London, 1932.
The central document.

AUERBACH, ERICH, *Mimesis: The Representation of Reality in Western Literature*, trans. Willard Trask, Princeton, 1953.
A major study of the operation of the various kinds of *mimesis* in specific works.

BALDWIN, T. W., *Shakespere's Five-Act Structure*, Urbana, Illinois, 1947.
Invaluable in tracing the traditional aspect of the plotting of Shakespeare's early plays. A monument of classical and Renaissance learning.

BEATY, JEROME, *'Middlemarch' from Notebook to Novel*, Urbana, Illinois, 1960.
A reliable reconstruction of George Eliot's compositional process.

BECKER, GEORGE J., ed., *Documents of Modern Literary Realism*, Princeton, 1963.
A convenient collection of the major continental manifestos of realism.

BECKETT, SAMUEL, *Proust and Three Dialogues with Georges Duthuit*, London, 1965 (first published, 1931).
An incisive analysis of the control of Time in Proust's work.

BOOTH, WAYNE, 'Did Sterne Complete *Tristram Shandy?*' *Modern Philology*, XLVII (1951), pp. 172–83. One of the more intelligent discussions of this mysterious subject.

BOOTH, WAYNE, *The Rhetoric of Fiction*, Chicago, 1961.
An interesting experiment in fiction.

BRADBURY, MALCOLM, 'Towards a Poetics of Fiction: 1) An Approach through Structure', *Novel*, I (1967), pp. 45–52.
A plea for detail, unusual for this journal.

CONRAD, JOSEPH, *Joseph Conrad on Fiction*, ed. Walter F. Wright, Lincoln, Nebraska, 1964.
A writer's indispensable account.

CRANE, R. S., 'The Concept of Plot and the Plot of Tom Jones', reprinted in *Perspectives on Fiction*, ed. J. L. Calderwood and H. E. Toliver, London, 1968, pp. 303–18.
The classic modern essay on plot.

CURTIUS, ERNST ROBERT, *European Literature and the Latin Middle Ages*, trans. Willard Trask, New York, 1953.
Chapter 5 on *topoi* is of particular interest.

DRYDEN, JOHN, 'An Essay of Dramatick Poesie, (1668)', in *Essays of John Dryden*, ed. W. P. Ker, Oxford, 1900, Vol. I, pp. 28–108.
A summary of neo-classical rules.

ELIADE, MIRCEA, *The Myth of the Eternal Return*, trans. Willard Trask, New York, 1954.
The anthropological source of the phrase *illud tempus*.

FOCILLON, HENRI, *The Life of Forms in Art*, New York, 1948.
A complex description of art in time and action.

FORSTER, E. M., *Aspects of the Novel*, London, 1927.
An essay which tries to separate 'story' from 'plot'.

FREEDMAN, RALPH, *The Lyrical Novel: Studies in Hermann Hesse, André Gide, and Virginia Woolf*, Princeton, 1963.
Introduces the phrase 'lyrical novel' and explains its validity.

FRIEDMAN, ALAN, *The Turn of the Novel*, New York, 1966.
Introduces the term 'stream of conscience'.

FRIEDMAN, NORMAN, 'Norms of the Plot', *Journal of General Education*, VIII (1955), pp. 241–53.

FRIEDMAN, NORMAN, 'Point of View in Fiction: The Development of a Critical Concept', *Publications of the Modern Language Association*, LXX (1955).

This article is especially important for the bibliography it contains of all modern criticism of the novel up to 1955.

FRYE, NORTHROP, *Anatomy of Criticism: Four Essays*, Princeton, 1957.

FRYE, NORTHROP, 'Myth, Fiction, and Displacement', in *Fables of Identity: Studies in Poetic Mythology*, New York, 1963, pp. 21–38.

Frye's work is semi-Aristotelian, but tries to extend the vocabulary of classicism into new areas.

GARRETT, PETER K., *Scene and Symbol from George Eliot to James Joyce*, New Haven, Conn., 1969.

A creative essay on the developments which take place between nineteenth and twentieth century fictions.

GIDE, ANDRÉ, *Journal des Faux-Monnayeurs*, Paris, 1927.

A moment-to-moment account of the gestation of *Les Faux-Monnayeurs*.

HORACE, *Ars Poetica*, Loeb edition, London, 1926.

One of the standard classical documents.

JAMES, HENRY, *The Art of the Novel*, ed. R. P. Blackmur, New York, 1935.

A reprinting of James's prefaces. Of major importance.

JAMES, HENRY, *The Art of Fiction*, in *The Portable Henry James*, ed. Morton Dauwen Zaubel, New York, 1951, pp. 391–418.

James's standard critical work.

HEIDEGGER, MARTIN, *Being and Time*, trans. John Macquerrie and Edward Robinson, Oxford, 1967.

Introduces and illustrates the idea of temporality.

HUMPHREY, ROBERT, *Stream of Consciousness in the Modern Novel*, California, 1962.

Clarifies the terminology of stream of consciousness writing.

KER, W. P., *Epic and Romance: Essays on Medieval Literature*, London, 1897.
An historico-literary study

KERMODE, FRANK, *The Sense of an Ending*, London, 1967.
A thorough study of literature in terms of time theories.

KERNAN, ALVIN B., *The Plot of Satire*, New Haven, Conn., 1965.
A study of the geometry of plot in satirical forms of the eighteenth and twentieth centuries.

LANGER, SUZANNE K., *Feeling and Form*, London, 1953.
Introduces new vocabulary and ideas to the idea of mechanical plotting.

LEAVIS, F. R., *The Great Tradition*, London, 1948.
Should be read by everyone interested in plot.

LESSER, SIMON O., *Fiction and the Unconscious*, New York and London, 1960.
A Freudian analysis.

LIDDELL, ROBERT, *Some Principles of Fiction*, London, 1953.
Illustrates a vague, general interest in fiction.

LUBBOCK, PERCY, *The Craft of Fiction*, London, 1921.
The first book to acclaim the concept of point of view in writing.

MCLUHAN, MARSHALL, *The Gutenberg Galaxy*, London, 1962.
An account of the change from linear comprehension to electronics.

MANN, THOMAS, *Die Enstehung des Doktor Faustus*, Amsterdam, 1949.
An account, both philosophical and practical, of the making of *Dr Faustus*.

MILLER, J. HILLIS, *Poets of Reality*, Cambridge, Mass., 1965.
A major study of the relationship of the writer to his and our fictions.

MUIR, EDWIN, *The Structure of the Novel*, London, 1928.
A latter-day examination of 'plot'.

PAULSON, RONALD, *The Fictions of Satire*, Baltimore, Maryland, 1967.
A study of satire which denies the old bases of plot.

POULET, GEORGES, *Etudes sur le Temps Humain* (Paris, 3 vols., 1953–64). Trans. Elliott Coleman, Baltimore, Maryland, 1956.
A literary study of time's contacts with history.

ROBBE-GRILLET, ALAIN, *Snapshots and Towards a New Novel*, trans. Barbara Wright, London, 1966.
A representative document of the 'nouveau roman' school.

RYMER, THOMAS, *A Short View of Tragedy*, London, 1693.
The criticism of a neo-classical crank.

SCHOLES, ROBERT AND KELLOGG, ROBERT, *The Nature of Narrative*, New York, 1966.
An attempt to re-classify narrative forms.

SIDNEY, SIR PHILIP, *An Apology for Poetry*, ed. Geoffrey Shepherd, London, 1965.
Renaissance absorption and development of Aristotle, Plato, Horace and the Cinquecento Italians.

SPINGARN, J. E., *A History of Literary Criticism in the Renaissance*, London, 1899.
An account of neo-classical ideas in Italy, France and England in the early Renaissance.

SWEDENBERG, H. T., JR., *The Theory of the Epic in England, 1650–1800*, California, 1944.
As its title suggests, a handbook.

TOLSTOI, LEO, *Tolstoi on Shakespeare*, trans. anon., Christchurch, Hants., 1907.
An interesting study in pre-socialist *mimesis*.

TRILLING, LIONEL, *The Liberal Imagination*, New York, 1950.
Projects the future of the mimetic form.

VAN GHENT, DOROTHY, *The English Novel: Form and Function*, New York, 1953.

Individual analyses of English and continental novels.

WEINBERG, BERNARD, *A History of Literary Criticism in the Italian Renaissance*, 2 vols., Chicago, 1961.

An impressive account of the critical developments in Italy during the Renaissance.

WHARTON, EDITH, *The Writing of Fiction*, New Haven, Conn., 1925.

A writer's handbook.

WOLFF, SAMUEL LEE, *The Greek Romances in Elizabethan Prose Fiction*, New York, 1912.

An interesting and convenient historico-literary account.

Index

Index